CASH FLOW MULTI-FAMILY INVESTING

The Definitive Guide to Investing in Multi-Family Properties

BY KEVIN MILLS

INTRODUCTION

There were many things that lead me to investing in multi-family real estate. Ultimately though, what made it a clear choice for me is that it just makes solid investing sense. My multi-family investments provide a solid income grow my portfolio year after year. It is a decision that I've never regretted making and a decision that I credit for my investing success and passion for real estate investing. It was a strategy I decided upon and learned on my own. I wish someone had told me about it and taken the time to walk me through it with me.

Investing in multi-family properties is a strategy that I whole heartedly recommend to investors that are ready to get serious about real estate investing. If that is you, I've written this book to provide you a step by step guide to multi family real estate investing.

Real estate investment has been responsible for creating more real wealth than any other investment strategy ever. Investing in real estate has been one of the most popular investment strategies for a long time, centuries. Investing in multi family properties is how investors get serious with their investment efforts and returns on their investments.

The benefits of investing in real estate include long-term appreciation, passive income, and tax advantages. However, investing in real estate is not always straightforward, and different types of properties require different investment approaches. Multi-family real estate investing has emerged as a popular investment option among investors looking for stable and profitable investments.

Multi-family real estate refers to residential properties that contain more than one unit, such as apartments, townhouses, or condominiums. Investing in multi-family real estate offers many benefits, including economies of scale, diversified cash flow, and tax benefits. Moreover, multi-family real estate investments tend to be more resilient to market downturns, making them an attractive option for investors seeking long-term stability.

Investing in multi-family real estate requires a different approach than investing in single-family homes. Multi-family properties have unique characteristics that require careful consideration when making investment decisions. For example, multi-family properties often require more management than single-family homes, and the cash flow generated from multi-family properties is different than that generated by single-family homes. Additionally, there are different strategies for investing in multi-family properties, such as direct ownership, real estate investment trusts (REITs), and syndication's.

In this book I will endeavor to provide a comprehensive guide to investing in multi-family real estate, including the benefits and risks associated with this type of investment. We will explore different strategies for investing in multi-family properties and the advantages and disadvantages of each. This book will provide insights into how to analyze multi-family properties, assess their profitability, and make informed investment decisions as well as what you will need to know to own and manage these types of properties.

The first section of this book covers the benefits of investing in multi-family real estate. It will provide an overview of the unique characteristics of multi-family properties and why they are an attractive investment option. In these sections we will also cover the different types of multi-family properties and the various ways to invest in them.

The second section of this book will cover the risks associated with investing in multi-family real estate. It will provide an overview of the potential risks and pitfalls of investing in multi-family properties, including market risk, property management risk, and financing risk. The section will also cover strategies for mitigating these risks and protecting your investment.

The third section of this book will cover the different strategies for investing in multi-family properties. It will provide an overview of direct ownership, REITs, and syndication's and the advantages and disadvantages of each. The section will also cover how to evaluate each strategy and determine which is best suited for your investment goals.

The fourth section of this book will cover the process of analyzing multi-family properties. It will provide a step-by-step guide to analyzing properties, including how to evaluate the property's location, market demand, and financial s. The section will also cover the different tools and resources available to help you analyze multi-family properties.

The fifth section of this book will cover the process of acquiring and managing multi-family properties. It will provide an overview of the different financing options available for multi-family properties, including traditional financing, private financing, and government financing. The section will also cover the process of managing a multi-family property, including tenant screening, property maintenance, and lease management.

Whether you are a seasoned real estate investor or a newcomer to the industry, this book will provide you with the knowledge and tools needed to successfully invest in multi-family real estate. From finding the right property to financing, managing, and maximizing your returns, this book will guide you through every step of the investment process. So, let's dive in and discover the exciting world of multi-family real estate investing!

CHAPTER ONE

Introduction to Multi Family Properties Investing

Multi family real estate investment is one of the most popular forms of investment amongst investors who are seeking to build real wealth and generate a regular passive income over time, to grow a portfolio of performing assets and even build generational wealth.

In my consulting practice, I often recommend that investors begin to start working their way into multi-family properties as an investment strategy as soon as they can or as soon as they are comfortable doing so. We also recommend that they start acquiring one or more properties with the intention of handing them down to their children to start building generational wealth, as a way to get their children involved and educated in real estate investing and provide them with a jump start their investing.

I encourage them to make their child part of the entire process. Take them to the property, let them know that it is theirs and someday, when they become an adult, they will be responsible for owning and running the building as profitable business. Show them how to do this. Teach them how to manage the property and then when thy are an adult, they have an income generating asset with equitable value.

Multi-family real estate investment is one of the most profitable and rewarding forms of real estate investment. Part of being an educated investor is making the most out of every investment and multi-family investments provide so many opportunities to do just that.

Why Multi-Family Properties?

Multi-family properties are residential buildings that contain more than one unit. These include duplexes, triplexes, townhouses and apartment buildings. Multi-family real estate investment has the potential for higher cash flow, greater appreciation, and the economies of scale, which are some of the key advantages of investing in multi-family properties over single family properties. It is important to remember that multi-family properties are businesses and they need to be acquired, held and managed like businesses to maximize the returns and benefits from them.

In this chapter we'll cover some of the principle benefits of multi-family real estate investing, the different types of multi-family properties, key metrics to consider when analyzing a potential investment, and the strategies for financing and managing a portfolio of properties.

One of the reasons I love investing in multi-family real estate is that it offers several advantages over other forms of real estate investment, like single-family homes or commercial properties.

Multi-family properties, also known as apartment buildings and even complexes when you have multiple structures with units in them as part of the same property, have become a cornerstone of the real estate industry. These properties provide housing for multiple families in one location, offering numerous benefits to both tenants and property owners. From the financial stability of consistent rental income to the convenience and affordability of shared amenities, multi-family properties are an essential and integral part of the housing market that are not going to be going away.

One of the greatest benefits of multi-family properties is their ability to generate consistent rental income for the property owners. Rather than relying on a single tenant to pay rent, such as in a single family property, multi-family properties can house multiple tenants, providing a more stable and reliable source of income. This consistent cash flow allows property owners to better plan and invest in their properties, making improvements and upgrades that benefit both the tenants, themselves and the community as a whole.

Another advantage of multi-family properties is the convenience and affordability of shared amenities. For example, many apartment buildings offer amenities such as gyms, swimming pools, and laundry facilities that would be too expensive for individual tenants to afford. Shared spaces like courtyards and common areas allow tenants to socialize and build a sense of community, something that can be difficult to find in single-family homes.

Multi-family properties also play a critical role in addressing the ongoing issue of affordable housing. By providing more housing units in one location, multi-family properties help alleviate the pressure on housing markets, making it more affordable for families to find a place to live. This is particularly important in areas where housing prices are high or there is a shortage of available housing. In a later chapter, we will cover the different types of affordable and government housing and the pros and cons of each.

Multi-family properties offer property owners the ability to diversify their real estate portfolio, spreading their investments across multiple units and locations. This helps mitigate the risk of market fluctuations and provides a level of stability and security for property owners.

Multi Family Property Types

It is pretty easy to figure out whether you are looking at a multi-family property or not. Essentially, if the property can legally house more than one rent paying, residential tenant, it is considered a multi-family property. Pretty simple right? Below are the common different types of multi-family properties and the simple descriptions of each.

Duplex

A duplex is a building with two separate residential units that consists of two separate housing units within that single structure. It is designed to accommodate two different and distinct residential rent paying tenants, each living in their own distinct living space while sharing a common wall, or floor. This type of housing arrangement is commonly found in urban or suburban areas and offers several advantages.

Inside each unit, you can expect to find a layout similar to a traditional home, including living areas, bedrooms, bathrooms, a kitchen, and possibly additional rooms such as a dining area, study, or laundry room. The interior spaces are generally designed to provide comfort and functionality for the residents.

Privacy is also an important consideration in multi-family duplexes. The shared wall or floor between the units is typically constructed with soundproofing materials to minimize noise transmission and ensure a comfortable living environment for both households.

The exterior of the multi-family duplex often includes outdoor spaces for each unit. Sometimes these outdoor areas a separated and other times they are shared. This can include private yards, patios, or balconies, allowing residents to enjoy outdoor activities and create their own personal oasis.

Overall, a multi-family duplex offers the benefits of shared expenses, privacy, and independence within a single structure. It provides an efficient use of space while offering the comfort and convenience of a home, making it an attractive choice for families or individuals seeking affordable and flexible housing options.

Triplex

A multi-family triplex is a residential building consisting of three separate housing units within a single structure. It is designed to accommodate three families or households, each occupying their own distinct living space. Multi-family triplexes are commonly found in urban or suburban areas and offer a range of benefits for residents.

The exterior of a multi-family triplex typically exhibits a balanced design, with three individual entrances and a shared wall or floor dividing each unit. The building can be one or multiple stories tall, depending on the design and local regulations. Each unit generally has its own private entrance, providing a sense of autonomy and privacy.

Inside each unit, just as in a Duplex, you can expect to find a layout similar to that of a traditional home. Each unit typically comprises living areas, bedrooms, bathrooms, a kitchen, and possibly additional rooms such as a dining area, study, or laundry room. The interior spaces are designed to offer comfort, functionality, and a sense of home for the residents.

Multi-family triplexes offer several advantages. First and foremost, they provide housing options for three separate and distinct rent paying tenants within a single structure, making efficient use of space.

As with a Duplex and all other multi-family properties, privacy is also an important consideration in triplexes. The shared walls and floors between units are typically constructed with soundproofing materials to minimize noise transmission and ensure a comfortable living environment for all residents. Each unit usually has its own separate utilities, further enhancing privacy and independence.

Outdoor spaces in multi-family triplexes can vary depending on the design and available land. Each unit may have its own designated outdoor area, such as a backyard, patio, or balcony, allowing residents to enjoy outdoor activities and create a personal outdoor space or it may be a shared area.

Fourplex

A multi-family fourplex is a residential building that consists of four separate housing units within a single structure. It is designed to accommodate four different and distinct rent paying tenants, with each unit occupying its own distinct living space. Multi-family fourplexes are commonly found in urban or suburban areas and offer several advantages for residents.

Inside each unit, you can expect to find a layout similar to that of a typical home. Each unit usually includes living areas, bedrooms, bathrooms, a kitchen, and additional rooms such as dining areas, studies, or laundry rooms. The interior spaces are designed to offer comfort, functionality, and a sense of home for the residents.

As with all multi-family properties, privacy is a key consideration in multi-family fourplexes. The building design typically includes soundproofing measures, such as insulated walls and floors to minimize noise transmission between units and ensure a comfortable living environment for all residents. Each unit is equipped with its own utilities, further enhancing privacy and independence.

Outdoor spaces in multi-family fourplexes can vary depending on the design and available land. Each unit may have its own designated outdoor area, such as a backyard, patio, or balcony, providing residents with opportunities to enjoy outdoor activities or create their own personal outdoor retreats.

Small Apartment Complex

A small apartment complex typically has between five and 50 units. Small apartment complexes provide more significant cash flow than smaller multi-family properties.

These buildings are designed to provide housing options for multiple different and distinct rent paying tenants within a compact and efficient footprint. Small apartment buildings are commonly found in urban or suburban areas and offer several advantages for residents.

Inside the small apartment building, you can expect to find a range of apartment sizes and layouts. Each apartment typically includes a living area, one or more bedrooms, and bathrooms, and a kitchen. The interior spaces are designed to maximize functionality and optimize the available square footage, providing comfortable living areas for the residents.

Small apartment buildings offer several benefits. Firstly, they provide multiple housing units within a single structure, making efficient use of space. This can be particularly advantageous in areas with high population density or where land availability is limited. Small apartment buildings can offer a cost-effective solution for individuals or families looking for affordable housing options.

Moreover, small apartment buildings often provide greater amenities and shared spaces for residents. These may include communal areas such as a swimming pool, gym, laundry facilities, or outdoor spaces like a courtyard or rooftop terrace. These shared amenities foster a sense of community and provide opportunities for social interaction among the residents.

Small apartment buildings also offer convenience and security. Many buildings are equipped with features such as secure entry systems, surveillance cameras, and on-site property management. These measures help ensure the safety and well-being of the residents.

Furthermore, small apartment buildings often benefit from convenient locations. They are frequently situated in close proximity to essential services, public transportation, shopping centers, and recreational facilities, offering residents easy access to a variety of amenities and activities.

Large Apartment Complex

A large apartment complex is a residential development that comprises a substantial number of individual apartment units within a single complex. These complexes are designed to accommodate a significant number of different and distinct rent paying tenants and are typically found in urban or suburban areas. A large apartment complex offers a range of amenities, services, and features that cater to the needs and preferences of its residents.

Inside the large apartment complex, there is a diverse selection of apartment units with various sizes, configurations, and floor plans. The units typically include living areas, multiple bedrooms, one or more bathrooms, a kitchen, and sometimes additional amenities such as a balcony or terrace. The interior spaces are designed to offer comfort, functionality, and modern living features to cater to the residents' needs.

One of the key advantages of a large apartment complex is the wide range of amenities and services it offers. These may include fitness centers, swimming pools, sports courts, children's play areas, landscaped gardens, communal spaces, business centers, and social areas like lounges or clubhouses. Additionally, some complexes may provide services such as on-site maintenance, concierge services, package delivery, or 24/7 security to enhance convenience and resident satisfaction.

Location is another significant factor in large apartment complexes. They are often strategically situated in areas with convenient access to transportation, schools, shopping centers, entertainment venues, and other essential amenities. This ensures that residents have easy access to the services and activities they require for a comfortable and enjoyable lifestyle.

Large apartment complexes are sought-after housing options for individuals and families looking for convenience, modern amenities, and a vibrant community atmosphere.

There are some other types of properties such as mixed-use and live-work space that also fall into these multi-family designations. Just remember, if it legally accommodates more than one different and distinct rent paying residential tenant, it is considered a multi-family property.

Economies of Scale

Now that we've gotten the basics out of the way, let's get into Economies of Scale. Economies of scale is an amazing thing and the greatest driving factor in multi-family profitability. It is one of my favorite factors in investing and in many of the businesses I have. Since it is a foundational element in multi-family real estate investing, it is key that we understand how it works and how it drives potential income from multi-family real estate investments.

Economies of scale refers to the cost advantages that a business can achieve by increasing production. It simply means, as a business produces more, the cost per unit decreases. This is because fixed costs, such as rent and salaries, can be spread out over a larger number of units, reducing the cost per unit. Multi-family properties benefit from economies of scale in several ways.

Multifamily properties have shared costs, such as utilities, property management, and maintenance. When you have multiple units in one building, these costs can be spread out over all of the units, reducing the cost per unit. For example, if you have a 10-unit building, the fixed cost of things like landscaping, pool care and other similar expenses will be less per unit than if you had 10 different single-family homes.

When you have multiple units in one building, you can take advantage of bulk purchasing. This means that you can negotiate with vendors for lower prices on supplies, such as paint, flooring, and appliances. By buying in bulk, you can save money on each unit, increasing your overall profitability.

When you have multiple units in one building, you can increase efficiency in several ways. For example, you can streamline maintenance and repair processes by having a dedicated team that can quickly respond to issues in any unit. This can reduce downtime, minimize disruptions for tenants, and ultimately save money on repairs and maintenance.

Now that we've discussed the ways in which multifamily properties benefit from economies of scale, let's explore how investors can take advantage of these benefits to increase their returns.

Investors can take advantage of economies of scale by investing in capital expenditures that will improve the property and attract higher-paying tenants. For example, upgrading appliances, adding amenities like a fitness center or pool, or renovating units can attract higher-paying tenants and increase cash flows. Keep in mind, many of these improvements apply to every unit in the building so capital investments go a long way to improving the over all value and income potential of multi-family property's.

Investors can also take advantage of economies of scale by outsourcing maintenance and repairs to third-party vendors. This can reduce labor costs and minimize downtime, allowing tenants to remain in their units and continue paying rent.

Economies of scale plays an important role in multi-family properties, offering cost advantages that can increase profitability and improve overall returns. By taking advantage of shared costs, bulk purchasing, and increased efficiency, investors can maximize their returns and generate long-term wealth. Effective property management, strategic capital expenditures, and outsourcing can all help investors take advantage of economies of scale and maximize the potential of their multifamily properties.

Cash Flow

Now that we understand Economies of Scale, let's talk about the money. Isn't that really why we do any of this? Cash flow is the income potential that investing in multi-family properties can provide us as investors.

If we're being honest, our likely motivations for investing in anything, including multi-family real estate boils down to income. How much money will this investment put into my pocket? Multi-family properties have the potential for higher cash flow than single-family homes because there are multiple units generating rental income. This can provide a steady stream of passive income for investors, making it an attractive investment opportunity.

Cash flow is a key factor in investing in multi-family properties and certainly our motivating factor and it should be. A property that doesn't cash flow is not a good investment and not something we should be wasting out time or money on.

Cash flow from multi family properties comes from the rental income generated by the tenants as well as any potential profit centers that are part of the property.

When investing in multi-family properties, it is important to understand the different sources of cash flow. One source of cash flow is the rental income from tenants. This income can be used to pay for operating expenses, such as property management, maintenance, property tax and repairs. The excess income can be used to pay down the mortgage or to generate a profit for the investor and if you're investing right, it will do both.

Another source of cash flow for multi-family properties are Cash Flow Centers. Cash flow centers are anything associated with the property that generates income that is additional to rents. This can be things like coin operated laundry machines, drink and snack machines or it could be services such as allowing tenants to pay for additional storage, parking spaces and other similar services. Income from these additional profit centers boosts your income by adding to your rental income. Don't just assume though that any profit center is a good fit for any property. For example, the lease and maintenance cost for a coin operated washer and dryer for a duplex might easily exceed any income benefit from having these machines in a duplex.

Evaluating Cash Flow

Pay attention to this part, it is very important. When you are evaluating a property, you absolutely must evaluate the actual and projected cash flow from any property we are considering.

When evaluating the cash flow potential of a multi-family property, it is essential that we consider the operating expenses and the gross income and that we know the actual costs of our expenses which typically include our mortgage payments, property taxes, insurance, utilities, maintenance, repairs, vacancy factor and property management fees. Expenses can significantly impact the cash flow of the property, and should be carefully evaluated to ensure that the property will generate a positive cash flow. It is also essential that every cost factor and potential cost factor be evaluated and considered.

Net Operating Income, Net Operating Cost and Net Profit

Lets break this down and even put it into a formula. You are going to add all of the gross income from the rents and add it to the gross income of any profit centers that you have. This is called the Gross Rents or Net Operating Income or NOI. Next, you are going to add up all of our costs, property taxes, insurance, utilities, maintenance, repairs, vacancy factor and property management fees. You also need to remember any costs associated with your profit centers. These could include but are not limited to the costs of equipment leases, maintenance and supplies. Some properties may have other expenses, some might not have every expense listed here. Make sure you know and account for each of the expenses that apply to your investment property. This is your Net Operating Cost or NOC, sometimes called Net Operating Expenses. Your Net Operating Costs account for the total cost to own, hold and operate the property. The Net Operating Income, minus the Net Operating Costs equals your Net Profit (NP) from the multi-family investment.

Here is that simple formula.

$$NOI - NOC = NP$$

As investors, you will run this formula as yearly cumulative numbers. The yearly cumulative of our NOI and the yearly cumulative of our NOC for our yearly cumulative NP.

Before you acquire any multi-family property, you will use this formula to determine whether or not the property you are considering will be a cash flowing property or not. The current owner of the property you are considering will provide the documentation of what the actual rental income is and what their actual costs are. In investing, these are know as the Actual numbers. Scrutinize the numbers provided to you and make sure they account for the actual rents being paid and the actual costs being paid. Take every possible factor into account. For example, what the current owner is paying for maintenance may be lower than what you will have to pay because they have a relationship with the maintenance company stretching back for years, even decades. This is just one example.

Pro Forma and Projected numbers are not Actual numbers but you need to understand them and how they affect your multi-family investments. Pro Forma is what someone believes the numbers should be based upon their opinion of what rents could be and how possible costs could be trimmed. For example, perhaps the current owner hasn't raised the rents in the past 5 years. Pro Forma numbers speculate what the market rents could be versus what the actual current rents are.

Projected numbers are what someone believes the numbers could be over time or after improvements or something that is a projected possibility. Running a projection is a good exercise. We know that rents will go up, we can calculate a reasonable projection of what that will be over the years. Maybe the property needs capital improvements which we know will make units in the building more desirable and drive up rents. Maybe there is a new project in the area that will drive up demand. These are scenarios that as investors you will take into account when considering projected rents for the future.

There are people who purchase properties based upon these speculations and there are those that have been very profitable in doing so. As a rule though, we should not be acquiring properties based on Pro Forma or Projected numbers alone. That said, if the actual numbers bear out a cash flowing property and we like what the Pro Forma and or Projected numbers offer, and we are confident that we have calculated every cost accurately, then we have a winner.

Consider this real world example. Disney purchased 60 acres in the Lake Nona area just South of Orlando Florida. In 2021, they announced that they were going to be building a new Billion dollar business campus on those 60 acres and relocating at least 2000 Imagineering employees from California to Florida in the next couple of years. Some Disney employees had already moved before 2021 was over. It was widely anticipated and announced that this project would pump Billions of dollars into the local economy and create a huge housing demand for the area. However, in 2023, Disney announced that it was cutting it's spending by 5.5 Billion dollars across the board and laid off over 7,500 employees. In May of 2023, Disney announced that they were not going to be moving forward with their previously planned Lake Nona project and employees would be staying in Southern California. Unfortunately, many investors had already flooded into the Lake Nona area buying up existing properties and land to build and develop new residential and commercial projects. If these investors purchased their properties based on actual numbers, they will still have cash flowing investments. However, if the actual numbers didn't support a cash flowing profile and they based their decision to purchase these investment properties solely upon projected incomes, they now own properties that are going to cost them money to own rather than making them money. The opportunity to get in on the ground floor can be a great but make sure your numbers still support a cash flowing profile.

You win some, you lose some, but don't lose your shirt. I have many personal experiences where I have purchased properties because a new campus or factory or something else that had been announced to be coming to a certain area. Then later for any number of different reasons those plans changed. The campus, factory or whatever else it was didn't get built or opened or in any way come to fruition. In each case, I made my purchases based upon actual numbers and I knew that there would be actual cash flow to provide profit. Would I have preferred to make a greater profit, of course I would have. Am I glad I didn't lose my shirt because I based my purchase on actual numbers and not the projections? You know it!!

You always want to use actual numbers. If you've run your numbers correctly, your NOI is greater than your NOC and you have a positive NP, you are looking at a cash flowing property. However, if your actual NOC's are greater than your NOI then your NP will be negative. This is clearly not an acquisition you should be considering. Always, make sure you know the actual numbers and use this formula. If the Actual numbers don't work, keep looking for a deal that has cash flow. There are many out there.

In the above formula, if you have a positive number for your Net Profit (NP), you have a property that is technically cash flowing. This is the profit that the business that is your multi-family investment makes for you every year. This is your pre-tax income.

Why do we call it "pre-tax" income? Because, depending upon how you receive this money, it will likely be considered income and you will have to pay income tax on it.

You will also use these formulas to calculate your annual ROI. ROI is Return On Investment. It is how much we make every year on our initial investment. We'll get into ROI later.

Overall, cash flow is and really really should be the most important consideration when investing in multi-family properties. By carefully evaluating the rental income, operating expenses, and potential for appreciation, investors can determine the potential cash flow of a property and make an informed investment decision.

Now that we understand the formula, let's get into understanding more about everything that goes into a multi-family real estate investment. Multi-family properties come in various types and sizes, ranging from small duplexes to large apartment complexes. Understanding the different types of multi-family properties can help investors make informed decisions when evaluating potential investments.

Higher Rental Income

One of the most significant advantages of investing in multi-family properties is the potential for higher rental income. With multiple units in one property, multi-family properties provide multiple streams of income, all built into one acquisition which can make them even more attractive for investors looking to generate passive income. This is even more true in areas with high demand for rental properties, where multi-family properties can generate significant cash flow.

Now lets talk about rent appreciation. Rents traditionally only go up. Even though rents can climb considerably, they rarely, if ever go back down. You should have a fixed rate on your loan or mortgage which means your mortgage payments aren't going to go up. Your property taxes and other costs will go up but they don't typically keep track with the rate of rental increases. Your rent should go up at least annually but certainly at the end of the tenants lease. If for example, your rents increase 5% annually, that is a 5% annual increase every year for your profits. That is a compounded annual profit of over 40% in just 5 years What this means for multi-family real estate investors is that, whatever their cash flow is in their first year, it is very likely going to exponentially go up year after year.

Investing in multifamily properties offers several advantages, including the the very obvious potential for higher cash flows. By having multiple rental units, benefiting from the Economies of Scale, and taking advantage of appreciation, investors can maximize their returns. By increasing rent, reducing expenses, and refinancing, investors can generate even more income from their multifamily properties. Investing in multifamily properties is the smart financial decision for those looking to generate passive income and building long-term wealth.

Appreciation

We already covered rent appreciation but another benefit of investing in multi family properties is Property Appreciation. Property Appreciation is the increase in the value of the multi-family property over time. Real estate naturally appreciates over time but there are other factors such as improvements to the property, changes in the local real estate market, or changes in the economy that also drive appreciation. Appreciation can also be a significant source of cash flow for investors, as it can increase the value of the property and allow the investor to refinance or sell the property for a profit.

To be able to understand what the current situation is with any given property and what potential a particular multi-family property might have, you need to analyze a number of things. Fortunately for you as an investor, you have a number of different formulas to help you get towards making a decision. Analyzing potential multi-family real estate investments requires understanding key metrics that are used to evaluate properties. Investors should consider the following metrics when evaluating potential investments:

Capitalization Rate

The Capitalization Rate (cap rate) is a measure of the property's potential return on investment. It is calculated by dividing the net operating income (NOI) by the property's value. The higher the cap rate, the more profitable the investment. For this formula you are going to take the NOI that we discussed earlier and divide it by the Acquisition Cost (AC) of purchasing the property . The formula looks like this;

$$\text{NOI} \div \text{AC} = \text{cap rate}$$

The cap rate plays a bigger part in properties with more units rather than fewer. Browsing through cap rates is an easy way to identify potential properties that we want to consider for investing. Many multi-unit properties will be listed with the cap rate right in the headline. Lots of property owners and listing agents like to manipulate numbers and will provide a cap rate based on their own Pro Forma or Projected numbers or numbers just not based in reality at all. Many property owners and listing agents don't actually know how to calculate the cap rate for a property. Don't trust that the cap rate in a listing is correct or even calculated with the correct numbers. When you find a cap rate and a property that catches your eye, use this formula with the actual numbers to calculate the actual cap rate.

We often see property owners or listing agents use a projected down payment amount for the purchase of the property to calculate a cap rate. Sure, if an investor is putting 50% to 70% down on a property and they are calculating the cap rate on 30% to 50% of the purchase price, they can make numbers look good. First, a 50% to 70% down payment on a property isn't realistic and shouldn't be necessary just to give a property the appearance of a good returns. Also, it just doesn't work like that. A properties Capitalization Rate is based on the purchase price of the property including any costs that go into the acquisition of the property. This includes the down payment amount. Remember what I just said, there are a lot of people out there that don't know how to calculate a cap rate, don't really know what a cap rate is or they think that someone will believe the cap rate they created is a reality even if it isn't. Don't get caught in that trap.

There are formulas where we will use the actual amount of cash put into the deal to acquire the property, not the purchase amount but the amount out of pocket. We use these formulas to calculate the cash-on-cash (ConC) return and the return on investment (ROI), but not the cap rate.

Cash on Cash and Return on Investment

Cash on Cash return (ConC) and Return on Investment (ROI) is a measure of the cash income generated by the property relative to the cash invested. It is calculated by dividing the annual cash flow by the total cash invested. A higher cash-on-cash return or return on investment indicates a more profitable investment. These numbers are typically represented as a percentage but you can use the same formulas to calculate the actual dollar amount of return. These are very similar formulas for nearly the same thing but let's break each of them down. For your Cash on Cash return, you'll take the Net Profit (NP) from our earlier formula. You then take the amount that has been paid in cash, the down payment for the property or if it is an all cash deal, the amount that has been paid in cash. This amount is known as Equity (E) You will divide the Net Profit (NP) by the Equity (E) to calculate your Cash on Cash (ConC) return. The formula looks like this;

$$\textbf{NP} \div \textbf{E} = \textbf{Cash on Cash Return}$$

To calculate your Return on Investment (ROI) we use the Net Profit (NP) from the earlier formula and divide it by Equity (E) and take that amount and multiply it times 100 which will provide you with a percentage. Your formula looks like this;

$$\textbf{NP} \div \textbf{E} = \textbf{Cash on Cash Return X 100} = \textbf{ROI}$$

If you are looking for a key take away from all of these formulas, it should be this; the larger the number, or percentage, the better. Use these formulas to help you zero in on potential investments and always verify your source numbers and your math.

Gross Rent Multiplier

The gross rent multiplier (GRM) is a measure of the property's value relative to its rental income. It is calculated by dividing the property's value by the gross annual rental income. The lower the GRM, the more valuable the property is.

The gross annual rental income is the total rent received from all units or spaces within the property, including any additional income from amenities such as parking or laundry facilities. The property price is the total cost to acquire the property, including any associated fees or costs.

The resulting GRM number provides an estimate of how many years it would take for the property's rental income to equal the total cost of the property. A lower GRM is generally considered more favorable because it indicates that the property has a higher potential for generating income relative to its purchase price. The formula for calculating GRM is: Acquisition Cost (AC) of the property, divided by the Net Operating Income (NOI)

$$AC \div NOI = GRM$$

GRM is a useful tool for real estate investors to compare the profitability of different properties and to identify potential investment opportunities. However, it is important to note that GRM alone does not provide a complete picture of a property's financial potential and should be used in conjunction with other metrics such as net operating income, cash-on-cash return, and cap rate

Vacancy Rate

Vacancy Rate is something an investor will calculate as an expense. The vacancy rate is a measure of the percentage of units in a property that are unoccupied and for what period of time they are unoccupied. A lower vacancy rate indicates a higher demand for the property, making it a more attractive investment. A higher vacancy rate is a likely indication that there is less demand for rental units. You'll need to break vacancy factors down in two ways. You need to look at the actual vacancy rate for the property you are interested in and the actual vacancy rate for the market. You can get the actual vacancy rate from the seller of the property and you can do a quick search or ask a real estate professional in the area for the vacancy factor in the market for the property. It wouldn't be unusual for both of these numbers to be identical or really close. If there is a major difference in these two numbers, the investor needs to look closer. If the vacancy factor for the property is significantly lower than the market vacancy factor, you want to know why? Is there something about this particular property that makes it more desirable to renters? Is it in a unique location? Is there an aggressive marketing plan to get tenants to sign leases? Whatever it is, the investor needs to know. If the vacancy factor for the property is higher than the vacancy factor for the market, the investor also needs to know why? Are there units that are down too long for maintenance? Are rents too high? What is making this building or the units in this building less desirable for renters?

Once the investor knows the actual vacancy rate for the property, they will calculate this as a percentage and this number will need to be factored as a cost in determining NOI. This is called the Vacancy Factor although the terms Vacancy Rate and Vacancy Factor are used nearly interchangeably.

To calculate the vacancy rate, the number of vacant units is divided by the total number of units in the area, and the result is expressed as a percentage.

For example, if there are 100 total rental units in a given area and 10 of those units are currently vacant, the vacancy rate would be 10%. A high vacancy rate may lead to decreased rental prices as landlords compete for tenants, while a low vacancy rate may result in increased prices and a more competitive market for renters or buyers. The long term average vacancy rate in the U.S. is 7.29%

Debt Service Coverage Ratio

What is Debt Service Coverage Ratio? The Debt Service Coverage

Ratio (DSCR) is an important financial metric used to evaluate the financial health of a multi-family real estate investment and the ability of a property to generate sufficient income to cover its debt obligations. It is a ratio that compares the net operating income (NOI) of a property to its annual debt service payments. In this section we will explore what the DSCR is, how it is calculated, and why it is important for investors.

The DSCR is expressed as a ratio, typically ranging from 1 to 2. A DSCR of 1 means that the property is generating just enough income to cover its debt obligations, while a DSCR greater than 1 indicates that the property is generating more income than it needs to cover its debt obligations.

How is Debt Service Coverage Ratio calculated?

The DSCR is calculated by dividing the property's net operating income (NOI) by its annual debt service payments. The formula for calculating the DSCR is:

$$\textbf{NOI} \div \textbf{Annual Debt Service Payments} = \textbf{DSCR}$$

Why is Debt Service Coverage Ratio important for Multi-family real estate investments?

The DSCR is an important financial metric for multi-family real estate investments because it provides investors with a clear picture of the property's ability to generate sufficient income to cover its debt obligations. A DSCR of less than 1 means that the property is generating insufficient income to cover its debt obligations, which puts the property at risk of defaulting on its loans.

Lenders also use the DSCR to evaluate the risk of lending to a multi-family property. Lenders typically require a minimum DSCR of 1.25 or higher before they will consider lending to a property. A higher DSCR indicates that the property is generating more income than it needs to cover its debt obligations, which makes it a lower-risk investment.

Investors can also use the DSCR to compare different multi-family real estate investments and to evaluate the potential return on investment. A higher DSCR indicates that the property has the potential to generate more income, which can lead to a higher return on investment.

The Debt Service Coverage Ratio is a crucial financial metric for evaluating the financial health of a multi-family real estate investment. It provides investors with a clear picture of the property's ability to generate sufficient income to cover its debt obligations and is used by lenders to evaluate the risk of lending to a property. Investors should aim for a DSCR of at least 1.25 to ensure that the property is generating enough income to cover its debt obligations and to minimize the risk of defaulting on its loans.

Now that you have the formulas, remember that they are only as good as the numbers you put into them. If you fail to account for a cost or income factor, if you don't have accurate numbers, these formulas won't provide you with the correct information, answers that you need to make the right decisions on your multi-family property acquisitions. The right numbers are out there, you can find them. Do the analysis, do the research and make sure you have all of the numbers and the right numbers.

We already know that multi-family real estate investments are a lucrative and rewarding way to generate passive income and build long-term wealth. By understanding the benefits, types of properties, key metrics, and financing and management strategies, investors can make informed decisions when evaluating potential investments. However, it is important to remember that real estate investment carries risks and should be approached with caution. Investors should conduct thorough due diligence and seek professional advice before making any investment decisions. With careful planning and management, multi-family real estate investment can provide a stable and profitable investment opportunity for individuals seeking to build long-term wealth.

Now that you know the financial guidelines for how to find and determine when you've found a property that makes sense for you and your investment needs, the next step is acquiring that property. Multi-family real estate investment requires significant capital upfront, making financing an essential consideration for investors. Investors can secure financing through a variety of sources, including traditional banks, private lenders, or government-backed loans. When evaluating potential financing options, investors should consider the interest rates, terms, and fees associated with each option.

Purchasing a multi-family property can be more complex than buying a single-family home. One of the biggest challenges that investors face is financing. Fortunately, there are a variety of financing options available for multi-family investments. In this chapter we will briefly cover each of these options and go into great depth on each of these financing options and understanding them later in this book.

Any property between one to four units are considered residential properties and considered homes. In this two to four unit range, these properties can be purchased as single family homes. We'll briefly discuss the benefits and drawbacks of this approach, in this Chapter and go into greater detail in Chapter Four. We will discuss and cover owner-occupant multi-family mortgages on two to four units and more.

One of the great benefits of buying a two to four-unit multi-family home is that these properties can be purchased with the same types of loans as a single family home. Some other great benefits are that rental incomes from the other units in the property can be included in the buyers income for qualifying for the loan and no previous experience as a property owner or landlord is required to qualify for the loans. One of the best loans to consider and a loan that nearly every buyer qualifies for to some extent or another is a Fair Housing Administration (FHA) loan. I find myself often recommending this option to new investors and first time home buyers that might want to start off with a first home that is also an investment property. To qualify for an FHA loan, Housing and Urban Development (HUD), the parent of FHA, requires that buyers of multi-family homes need to occupy one of the units as their primary residence. With an FHA loan, investors only need to come up with a 3.5% down payment and are available to borrowers with lower credit scores than conventional loans. FHA loans have lower credit score requirements and lower down payment requirements. However, FHA loans have higher mortgage insurance premiums and stricter property standards. An FHA loan provides a great opportunity for buyers of two to four-unit multi-family properties to have rental income from their primary residence.

They can rent out the other units and use the rental income to pay their housing payments. There are instances where many owners of two to four-unit properties have their rental income pay for their mortgage and all other housing expenses. Some two to four-unit multi-family owners even have positive cash flow after paying all housing expenses.

There are other loans that investors planning to occupy one of the units can qualify. Fannie Mae (FNMA) and Freddie Mac (FHLMC) allows investment property financing on conventional loans. Conventional Loans require a 15% to 25% down payment on financing for investment properties two to four units.

VA Loans allow 100% financing on one to four-unit for owner-occupant properties. VA loans are available to eligible veterans and their families and are guaranteed by the Department of Veterans Affairs. These loans require no down payment and have more flexible credit requirements than conventional loans. VA loans have more flexible credit requirements and require no down payment. However, VA loans are only available to veterans and have stricter property standards than conventional loans. Additionally, VA loans are only available for properties with up to four units.

Conventional financing is a popular option for investors because it typically offers lower interest rates and more flexible terms than other types of financing. Additionally, conventional loans can be used to purchase a wide variety of multi-family properties, including those with up to four units. As you can see, there are many loan options for conventional financing of two to four unit multi-family investment properties. Speak with a mortgage professional and have them help you decide which one fits best for all of your needs.

Another benefit of conventional financing is that there is a wide range of options and conventional loans are easily available from a variety of lenders, including banks, credit unions, and mortgage brokers. This makes it easier for investors to shop around for the best rates and terms.

While conventional financing can be a great option for some

investors, it does have some drawbacks. One of the biggest challenges is that conventional loans typically require a higher down payment than other types of financing, such as FHA or VA loans. This can make it more difficult for investors to purchase a property, especially if they are just starting out.

Another potential challenge is that conventional loans may have stricter underwriting standards than other types of financing. This means that investors will need to have a strong credit history, a stable source of income, and a low debt-to-income ratio in order to qualify.

If you are interested in purchasing a multi-family property with conventional financing, there are several steps you can take to make the process smoother.

Get pre-approved before you start shopping for properties. It's a good idea to get pre-approved for a loan. This will give you a better idea of how much you can afford to spend and will make it easier to make offers on properties and will allow you a greater degree of confidence in making your offers.

Shop around for the best rates and terms. Rates and terms vary from lender to lender and mortgage broker to mortgage broker. Though it is usually a trade off, better terms mean higher rates, better rates mean more spent on terms to find a loan package that works for you and your needs. You may want to consider working with a mortgage broker who can help you compare offers from multiple lenders.

Be prepared for the underwriting process. Conventional loans typically require more documentation and scrutiny than other types of financing. Be prepared to provide a lot of paperwork, including tax returns, bank statements, and proof of income as well as actual incomes for the property being purchased to be considered as potential income.

Work with an experienced real estate agent that has experience with these types of multi-family purchases. Purchasing a multi-family property is a complex process, and it's important to work with a real estate agent who can help guide you through the process.

Purchasing a multi-family property with conventional financing can be a great way to build wealth and generate passive income. While it does come with some challenges, including stricter underwriting standards, the benefits of this type of financing can make it a worthwhile investment.

Properties 5 units and above don't qualify for conventional financing but that doesn't mean there aren't many options for finding and securing financing for these multi-family properties.

Portfolio loans are offered by banks and other financial institutions that hold the loans on their own balance sheets, rather than selling them to investors. These loans can be more flexible than conventional loans and may be available to borrowers with lower credit scores. Portfolio loans may offer more flexibility in terms of underwriting and may be available to borrowers with less than perfect credit. However, portfolio loans may have higher interest rates and require larger down payments than conventional loans.

Hard money loans are short-term, high-interest loans that are typically used by real estate investors to finance fix-and-flip projects or other short-term investments. These loans are typically offered by private lenders and have less strict credit requirements than other types of financing. Hard money loans offer flexible terms and can be an option for investors who need to close quickly. However, hard money loans have high interest rates and fees and may require a large down payment.

One of my personal favorite financing options is Seller Financing. The Seller Finance option is rare but you will find that the more you start acquiring multi-family properties and more you negotiate with multi-family sellers, though still rare, it will become easier to find and negotiate. Seller financing is an arrangement in which the seller of a property provides financing to the buyer. This can be a good option for investors who are unable to obtain traditional financing or who want to avoid the strict underwriting requirements of traditional loans. Seller financing can offer more flexibility in terms of underwriting and may require less documentation than traditional loans. However, seller financing may have higher interest rates than other types of financing and may require a large down payment.

When it comes to financing a multi-family investment property, there are several options available to investors. Each option has its own advantages and disadvantages, and the best option for you will depend on your personal financial situation and investment goals. It's important to carefully consider all of your options and work with a qualified lender to find the financing solution that best meets your needs. By doing your research and working with experienced professionals, you can successfully navigate the financing process and achieve your investment goals.

Another important factor to consider when investing in multi-family properties is property management. Managing a multi-family property can be challenging, especially if you are a new investor. You must ensure that the property is well-maintained, tenants are satisfied, and rent is collected on time. You can hire a property management company to handle these tasks, but this can significantly impact your cash flow.

Once the property is purchased, effective management is crucial to the success of the investment. Effective management includes managing tenant relations, maintenance and repairs, and financial reporting. Managing a multi-family property can be complex and time-consuming, especially for new investors. Investors can choose to manage the property themselves or hire a property management company to handle day-to-day operations. Property management companies can provide a range of services, including tenant screening, rent collection, and property maintenance. Property managers need to be skilled in handling tenant relationships, maintenance and repair issues, and financial reporting.

Before you dive into the market, it's important to understand the local multi-family real estate market. Every market is unique and has its own set of challenges and opportunities. In this chapter, we'll explore some key factors to consider when analyzing the local multi-family real estate market.

One of the most important factors to consider when analyzing the local multi-family real estate market is demographics. You'll want to research the area's population growth, job growth, and income levels. Areas with strong job growth and higher-than-average incomes are typically more desirable for multi-family investments, as they are more likely to attract tenants who can afford higher rents.

Another important factor to consider is the inventory of multi-family properties in the area. You'll want to research the number of units available, the average rent prices, and the vacancy rates. Areas with a high demand for rental housing and a low vacancy rate may be more favorable for multi-family investments.

You'll also want to research current market trends in the area. Are prices rising or falling? Is there a high demand for multi-family properties? Are there any new developments or construction projects in the works? Understanding market trends can help you make more informed investment decisions and identify opportunities for growth.

Local regulations can also have a big impact on the multi-family real estate market. You'll want to research zoning laws, building codes, and other regulations that may affect your ability to invest in the area. Some cities have rent control laws that may limit your ability to raise rents, while others may have restrictions on the number of units that can be built in a certain area.

Finally, you'll want to research the competition in the area. Who are your competitors? What are their strengths and weaknesses? How can you differentiate your property from theirs? Understanding your competition can help you identify opportunities for growth and ensure that your property is competitive in the market.

Understanding the local multi-family real estate market is crucial for making informed investment decisions. By researching demographics, inventory, market trends, local regulations, and competition, you can identify opportunities for growth and mitigate potential risks. It's important to work with experienced professionals, such as real estate agents and property managers, who have a deep understanding of the local market and can provide valuable insights into the investment potential of multi-family properties in the area. By doing your research and working with experienced professionals, you can successfully navigate the local multi-family real estate market and achieve your investment goals.

CHAPTER TWO

Market Analysis

Multi-family real estate investments have gained significant popularity, and for good reason. This asset class offers investors stable and predictable cash flow, long-term appreciation potential, and tax benefits. However, as with any investment, there are risks involved. To make informed investment decisions, it is essential to conduct a thorough market analysis. In this chapter, we will discuss the key factors that investors should consider when analyzing the multi-family real estate market.

If you're going to be serious about investing in multi-family properties, you need to be series about conducting a market analysis. Conducting a Market Analysis is a crucial step for investors who want to make informed decisions about multi-family real estate investments. By staying informed about the local economy, real estate market, competition, regulatory factors, and potential risks, investors can identify investment opportunities, determine property value, and mitigate potential risks and challenges associated with their investment.

A thorough market analysis can help investors maximize their investment returns and position themselves for success in the multi-family real estate market. Most investors choose to focus on market's they are familiar with and it is because they understand the market and by having investments in those markets, they keep up with market changes and trends. It is very possible that a market that is currently strong might change in the future and not be as great a market to invest in.

One example of these markets is Detroit. Detroit in the 1960's was the fourth most populous city in America. Now it is the 27th and is trending to drop even more. In the early 70's, Automotive manufacturers started moving their operations out of Michigan and to "Right To Work" states that weren't as controlled by unions and didn't require non union members to pay union dues. Now we know what Detroit looks like. If we'd been investors investing in the Detroit market, we should have hopefully seen these trends and gotten out of the market in time. That isn't to say there aren't still opportunities in Detroit. I personally know real estate investors that like investing in Detroit. Why? They've done their market analysis and figured out how their investing strategy works for them in that market.

Whether easy to define or not, are you able to find a strategy in a particular market that is profitable? As investors, we need to always be looking outside of the box. Often times, an outside of the box strategy will be profitable whereas an inside the box, conventional strategy may not be as profitable or profitable at all. Find a strategy that works for you. If you can't, find another market and start looking at strategies there.

Let's take a look at some steps that investors can follow to conduct a thorough market analysis for multi-family real estate investments:

Investors need to first identify the target market they want to invest in. This involves determining the geographic area and the demographic characteristics of the renters they wish to target. Understanding the target market can help investors tailor their investment strategy to meet the needs and preferences of their target renters.

Understanding the local economy is crucial for investors to determine whether there is a demand for multi-family properties in the target market. Investors must analyze factors such as job growth, population growth, and industry trends in the target market. These factors can help investors understand the rental demand for multi-family properties in the target market.

Investors must analyze the local real estate market to determine the supply and demand dynamics of multi-family properties in the target market. This includes analyzing factors such as vacancy rates, rental rates, and the supply of multi-family properties. Investors should also analyze trends in property values in the target market to determine the potential for capital appreciation.

Investors must analyze the competition in the target market to determine how their properties can compete effectively. This includes analyzing the rental rates, amenities, and services offered by comparable properties in the area. Investors should also analyze the location, quality, and occupancy rates of competing properties to determine their competitive advantage.

Investors must consider regulatory factors that may impact their investment, such as zoning regulations, tax policies, and rent control laws. These factors can impact the profitability of an investment in the multi-family real estate market. Investors should stay informed about changes in the regulatory environment and adjust their investment strategies accordingly.

Based on the market analysis, investors can determine the value of the property they wish to invest in. This involves analyzing the rental income potential of the property, the potential for capital appreciation, and the potential for cost savings through property improvements. Investors can use these factors to estimate the property's value and determine whether it is a profitable investment.

As an investor, you must assess potential risks associated with your investment, such as changes in the local economy or regulatory environment. you must also identify potential challenges associated with managing and operating the property, such as maintenance costs and tenant turnover. By identifying potential risks, investors can develop strategies to mitigate these risks and maximize their investment returns.

Demographic trends play a crucial role in the demand for multi-family housing. It's important to assess the population growth, household formation rates, age distribution, and migration patterns in a specific market. For example, cities with younger populations may have a higher demand for multi-family housing, while areas with an aging population may have a higher demand for senior housing. Investors should also consider the impact of population growth on the local economy and job market, as a growing population can drive demand for multi-family housing.

Demographic trends have a profound effect on the demand for housing, particularly multi-family housing. There are several demographic trends that have been observed in recent years, which are driving the demand for multi-family housing.

One of the most significant demographic trends is urbanization. Across many developed countries, there has been a shift towards urbanization, with an increasing number of people choosing to live in cities. This trend has been driven by a range of factors, including access to better job opportunities, improved infrastructure, and higher levels of education and healthcare. As more people move to cities, the demand for housing in urban areas has increased, and multi-family housing has become a popular choice for those who want to live in the city but cannot afford to buy a single-family home.

Another important demographic trend that is driving the demand for multi-family housing is the rise in single-person households. Across many developed countries, the number of people living alone has been steadily increasing. This trend is driven by various factors, including delayed marriage, divorce, and longer life expectancy. Single-person households typically require smaller living spaces and are more likely to choose multi-family housing, which offers affordable and convenient options. Multi-family housing can provide a range of amenities and services, including fitness centers, community spaces, and easy access to public transportation, which can be especially important for single-person households.

The aging population is also driving the demand for multi-family housing. As people age, they may choose to downsize their homes, either to save money or because they no longer need as much space. Multi-family housing provides a range of options for seniors, from independent living to assisted living, which can be more affordable and offer more amenities than traditional single-family homes. As the population continues to age, the demand for senior housing is likely to continue to increase. This is one of the segments that I and other investors have been giving increasing attention to.

Changes in household composition are also contributing to the demand for multi-family housing. Multi-generational households, where multiple generations of a family live under one roof, are becoming more common in many countries. These households often require larger living spaces and may prefer multi-family housing, which can accommodate multiple generations more easily. Multi-family housing can offer a range of options, from larger apartments to townhouses, which can be suitable for multi-generational households.

Immigration is another huge, major driver of demand for multi-family housing. Immigrants often have limited financial resources and may prefer to live in affordable multi-family housing, which can provide a sense of community and support. Additionally, multi-family housing is often located in urban areas, which can provide easier access to jobs, schools, and other services. As immigration patterns continue to change, the demand for multi-family housing is likely to continue to increase.

Demographic trends play a crucial role in the demand for multi-family housing. Urbanization, the rise in single-person households, the aging population, changes in household composition, and immigration patterns are all contributing to the increasing demand for affordable and convenient housing options. As these trends continue, it is likely that the demand for multi-family housing will remain strong, making it an important sector of the housing market for years to come.

Economic indicators can provide insight into the multi-family real estate market. It's important to analyze factors such as job growth, income levels, affordability, interest rates, inflation rates, and the overall health of the economy. Investors should consider the impact of job growth and income levels on the demand for multi-family housing, as areas with robust job markets and higher incomes may attract more renters seeking high-end multi-family housing options. Additionally, investors should assess the impact of interest rates on the housing market, as rising interest rates can lead to lower demand for homes and higher demand for rentals.

Economic indicators play a critical role in the performance of multi-family properties. Understanding how economic indicators can impact the demand for multi-family properties and their profitability is essential for investors in this sector.

Interest rates are one of the most important economic indicators affecting multi-family properties. When interest rates rise, borrowing money becomes more expensive, which can reduce the number of investors looking to purchase multi-family properties. This can lead to a decrease in demand for multi-family properties and a reduction in their value. Conversely, when interest rates are low, borrowing money becomes more affordable, which can increase demand for multi-family properties and their value.

Job growth is another critical economic indicator affecting the demand for multi-family properties. When there is job growth in a region, there is typically an increase in demand for housing in that region, including multi-family properties. This can lead to an increase in rental rates and occupancy rates for multi-family properties. Conversely, when job growth slows down or declines, the demand for housing in that region decreases, which can lead to a decrease in rental rates and occupancy rates for multi-family properties.

Gross domestic product (GDP) is also an essential economic indicator affecting multi-family properties. GDP measures the total value of goods and services produced within a country. When GDP is strong, there is typically an increase in job growth and consumer spending, which can have a positive impact on multi-family properties. This can lead to an increase in rental rates and occupancy rates for multi-family properties. Conversely, when GDP is weak, there is typically a decrease in job growth and consumer spending, which can have a negative impact on multi-family properties.

Inflation is another critical economic indicator affecting multi-family properties. When inflation is high, it can lead to an increase in the cost of living, including the cost of housing. This can lead to a decrease in demand for multi-family properties, as renters may be unable to afford the rental rates. Conversely, when inflation is low, it can lead to a decrease in the cost of living, including the cost of housing. This can lead to an increase in demand for multi-family properties, as renters may be able to afford the rental rates.

Other factors that can affect the performance of multi-family properties include government policies, tax incentives, and changes in zoning regulations. These factors can impact the supply and demand for multi-family properties, as well as their profitability. For example, government policies that encourage the development of affordable housing can increase the supply of multi-family properties, while tax incentives can increase their profitability.

Economic indicators have a significant impact on the performance of multi-family properties. Interest rates, job growth, GDP, and inflation are critical economic indicators affecting the demand for multi-family properties and their profitability. Understanding how these economic indicators impact the multi-family property market can help investors make informed decisions about their investments in this sector. Additionally, monitoring government policies, tax incentives, and changes in zoning regulations can help investors stay ahead of changes in the market and make strategic investment decisions.

Supply and demand dynamics are essential in the multi-family real estate market. Investors should analyze the supply and demand dynamics in a specific market to determine whether it is a good investment opportunity. Factors such as the number of existing properties, the age and condition of those properties, and the level of amenities they offer can impact the potential success of a new property. Additionally, investors should consider the level of competition from other types of housing, such as single-family homes or apartments. It's essential to understand the current and future demand for multi-family housing in a particular market to make informed investment decisions.

The multi-family real estate market is subject to complex and dynamic supply and demand dynamics that can greatly impact the performance of the market. Understanding how these dynamics operate is essential for investors who wish to make informed decisions in this market.

Supply is the total number of multi-family properties available on the market. The supply of multi-family properties can be influenced by a range of factors, such as new construction, property renovation, changes in zoning regulations, and property conversions. When the supply of multi-family properties increases, it can lead to a decrease in rental rates and occupancy rates. This can create more competition among landlords, which may negatively impact the profitability of multi-family properties.

Demand, on the other hand, refers to the total number of renters seeking multi-family properties. The demand for multi-family properties is driven by factors such as population growth, job growth, immigration, and changes in household composition. When demand for multi-family properties increases, it can lead to an increase in rental rates and occupancy rates, which can benefit the profitability of multi-family properties.

In order to fully understand the supply and demand dynamics in the multi-family real estate market, it is necessary to consider the factors that impact both supply and demand. For instance, new construction projects can increase the supply of multi-family properties, which can lower the occupancy and rental rates, negatively impacting the profitability of existing properties. Referring to the earlier example, this is what is likely going to happen to investors who invested in the Lake Nona area counting on the proposed Disney project that didn't go through.

Conversely, limited new construction, particularly in high-demand areas, can increase the demand for multi-family properties, resulting in higher occupancy and rental rates.

Another important factor that affects supply and demand is household composition. Demographic trends such as a rise in single-person households or multi-generational households can influence the demand for multi-family properties. For example, single-person households typically require smaller living spaces and may prefer multi-family housing, while multi-generational households may require larger living spaces and may prefer multi-family properties that can accommodate multiple generations.

The supply and demand dynamics in the multi-family real estate market are a critical factor for investors to consider. Understanding how factors such as new construction, household composition, and changes in zoning regulations can impact supply and demand is essential for making informed investment decisions. By monitoring these factors and anticipating changes in the market, investors can position themselves for success in the multi-family real estate market.

Competitive Landscape

Analyzing the competitive landscape is crucial when investing in multi-family real estate. Investors should assess the number and quality of existing properties in the market, as well as the level of amenities they offer. Investors should also consider the potential for new construction in the market, as new construction can impact the supply and demand dynamics. Investors must consider a range of factors that impact the competitive landscape of the market. Additionally, it's important to analyze the pricing strategies of existing properties, such as rental rates and incentives, to assess the potential profitability of a new investment. Understanding these factors is critical for making informed decisions about purchasing, managing, and operating multi-family properties.

Location is one of the most important factors that impact the competitive landscape of the multi-family real estate market. Properties in desirable locations, such as those close to major employment centers, entertainment districts, and transportation hubs, are more competitive and more in demand than those in less desirable locations. Investors must consider the location of their properties to determine how to position them to compete effectively in the market.

The quality of the property is another key factor that can impact its competitiveness in the multi-family real estate market. Properties that are well-maintained, have modern amenities, and offer a high standard of living are more competitive than those that are outdated or in need of repair. Investors must invest in high-quality materials, finishes, and appliances to differentiate their properties from the competition and command higher rental rates.

Rental rates are another critical factor in the competitive landscape of the multi-family real estate market. Understanding the rental rates of comparable properties in the area can help investors set appropriate rental rates for their properties. They must also consider the amenities and services offered by comparable properties and ensure that their properties offer competitive amenities and services to attract renters.

The amenities and services offered by a property can significantly impact its competitiveness in the multi-family real estate market. Amenities such as fitness centers, swimming pools, communal spaces, and parking can be crucial in attracting and retaining renters. Investors must consider the cost and feasibility of offering amenities and services that are in line with those offered by the competition.

Zoning Regulations

Changes in zoning regulations, new construction, and the availability of financing can also impact the competitive landscape of the multi-family real estate market. Changes in zoning regulations can make it easier or more difficult to build multi-family properties in certain areas. If zoning regulations become more restrictive, this can decrease the supply of multi-family properties and lead to an increase in rental rates. Investors must stay informed about these factors to anticipate changes in the market and adjust their strategies accordingly. For example, new construction in the area can increase the supply of properties and lead to decreased rental rates, while changes in zoning regulations can make it more difficult to develop new multi-family properties.

Zoning regulations are critical regulatory factor that can impact the profitability of an investment in the multi-family real estate market. Changes in zoning regulations can impact the ability of developers to construct new multi-family properties in certain areas, which can limit the supply of properties and increase the value of existing properties. Conversely, changes in zoning regulations that encourage the development of new multi-family properties can increase the supply of properties and decrease the value of existing properties.

Rent Control

Rent control laws are another regulatory factor that can impact the profitability of investments in the multi-family real estate market. Rent control laws regulate the amount that landlords can charge for rent and can limit the ability of landlords to increase rental rates.

Rent control laws can decrease the profitability of an investment by limiting the amount of rental income that landlords can earn. Another factor we see in markets with rent control is a decreased demand for purchases of these rent controlled properties.

Building codes are another critical regulatory factor that can impact the profitability of an investment in the multi-family real estate market. Building codes regulate the construction and safety standards of multi-family properties. Investors must ensure that their properties comply with building codes to avoid costly fines or legal issues that can negatively impact profitability.

In addition, there are other regulatory factors that can impact the profitability of an investment in the multi-family real estate market, such as zoning restrictions, environmental regulations, and fair housing laws. Investors must stay informed about these regulations and adjust their investment strategies accordingly.

To mitigate regulatory risks and maximize the profitability of their investments in the multi-family real estate market, investors must stay informed about the regulatory environment and understand the potential impacts of changes in regulations. They must also work with professionals such as attorneys, tax advisors, and property managers to ensure that they comply with regulations and mitigate risks associated with regulatory compliance. By doing so, investors can position themselves for success in the multi-family real estate market.

Taxes

One of the most significant regulatory factors that impact the profitability of investments in the multi-family real estate market is tax policies. Taxes can directly impact the profitability of an investment by increasing or decreasing the amount of taxes owed on rental income or capital gains and the taxes owed on your investment property. Changes in tax policies can significantly impact the profitability of an investment, and investors must stay informed about potential changes to these policies.

Conducting a thorough market analysis is critical for investors looking to invest in multi-family real estate. By analyzing demographic trends, economic indicators, supply and demand dynamics, the competitive landscape, and the regulatory environment, investors can assess the potential profitability of a particular investment opportunity. Additionally, it's important to stay up-to-date on market trends and economic indicators that may affect the multi-family real estate market in the future. Investors should take a data-driven approach and use available data to make informed investment decisions.

Market cycles in multi-family real estate investing are influenced by a variety of factors and can have a significant impact on investment performance. In addition to the economic indicators mentioned previously, other factors that can impact market cycles in multi-family real estate investing include demographic trends, urbanization patterns, and zoning regulations. For example, demographic trends such as an aging population or an increase in single-person households can impact the demand for multi-family housing. Similarly, urbanization patterns can impact the demand for multi-family housing in urban areas, whereas zoning regulations can impact the supply of new properties in certain areas.

One way to identify market cycles in multi-family real estate investing is to conduct market research to gain insights into local market conditions. This research can involve analyzing local real estate market data, rental rates, vacancy rates, and employment trends. By conducting this research, investors can gain a better understanding of how the market is likely to perform in the future and make more informed investment decisions.

Mitigating the effects of market cycles in multi-family real estate investing can also involve taking advantage of market opportunities. For example, during a market downturn, properties may be available at lower prices, providing investors with opportunities to acquire properties at a discount. Similarly, during an upswing in the market, investors can sell properties for a profit.

Another strategy for mitigating the effects of market cycles in multi-family real estate investing is to actively manage properties. This can involve improving property management, reducing expenses, and increasing revenue. By managing properties effectively, investors can improve cash flow and reduce the impact of market fluctuations on investment performance.

Finally, it's important to note that market cycles in multi-family real estate investing are not always predictable, and investors should be prepared to adapt their investment strategies as market conditions change. This may involve reevaluating investment goals, adjusting the portfolio mix, or changing investment strategies altogether.

Market cycles are an inevitable part of multi-family real estate investing, and understanding how they work is essential for successful investing. By conducting market research, taking advantage of market opportunities, actively managing properties, and being prepared to adapt investment strategies as needed, investors can mitigate the effects of market cycles and build a successful multi-family real estate investment portfolio.

CHAPTER THREE

Property Analysis

Once you've done your market analysis and settled on a market and a strategy or even a set of strategies you want to apply to your multi-family properties in that market, it's time to start identifying potential multi-family acquisitions. This is where you start focusing on specific properties to see if they meet your criteria for your investing strategies and profit margins. Property analysis is a critical component of multi-family real estate investing. It involves evaluating the financial, physical, and market characteristics of a specific, potential investment property to determine its potential profitability and minimize risk. In this chapter, we will discuss in detail the key factors to consider when conducting a property analysis for multi-family real estate investing.

The financial analysis of a multi-family property is an essential part of property analysis. It involves evaluating the actual financial statements of the property to determine its current and potential profitability. In Chapter One we went over the formulas for these key financial metrics to consider:

Net Operating Income (NOI)

The NOI represents the property's income minus its operating expenses, not including debt service. This metric is used to determine the property's potential profitability.

Capitalization Rate (Cap Rate)

The cap rate is calculated by dividing the property's NOI by its value. The cap rate represents the expected return on investment for the property.

Cash-on-Cash Return

This metric represents the annual cash flow generated by the property divided by the amount of equity invested.

Debt Service Coverage Ratio (DSCR)

The DSCR measures the property's ability to cover its debt obligations. A DSCR of 1.2 or higher is generally considered healthy.

Vacancy Rate

The vacancy rate reflects the property's occupancy levels. A high vacancy rate may indicate that the property is not performing well, while a low vacancy rate may suggest that there is strong demand for the property.

Other important financial factors to consider include the property's financing options, such as the interest rate, terms of the loan, and any prepayment penalties. These can impact the property's overall profitability.

The physical analysis of a multi-family property involves evaluating the physical condition of the property. This includes inspecting the buildings systems, such as electrical, plumbing, and HVAC systems, as well as the structural integrity of the property.

It is also important to assess the condition of the common areas, such as hallways, stairwells, and parking lots. These areas can impact the property's overall appeal to tenants and its ability to generate income.

The age, location, and amenities of the property are also important physical factors to consider. Older properties may require more maintenance and repairs, while properties located in desirable areas with access to public transportation and other amenities may command higher rents.

The market analysis of a multi-family property involves evaluating the local rental market to determine the demand for rental units in the area, as well as the prevailing rental rates and whether the units in the property are comparable to the other units available on the market. Are they as current and updated? Do they offer the same amenities. For example, do the units in the property you are considering have dishwashers and sky lights and most of the other units in the markets do not? If so, these would be factors that would make these units more desirable and more in demand. If on the other hand, most of the units on the market have dishwashers and sky lights and the ones in the property you are considering do not, this means they are less desirable than the other units on the market and will have less demand. Consider market factors such as parking, covered or uncovered parking, property amenities, common and community areas and any other factor that you can compare to other similar units and properties in the market.

Conducting a thorough property analysis is critical for successful multi-family real estate investing. The financial, physical, and market characteristics of the property should be carefully evaluated to determine its potential profitability and minimize risk. By conducting a comprehensive property analysis, investors can identify properties that offer strong potential for long-term growth and income. It is important to note that property analysis is an ongoing process, and investors should regularly evaluate the property's performance and make adjustments as needed to maximize its profitability.

Evaluating the property is a crucial step in multi-family real estate investing. Conducting a thorough evaluation of a potential investment property can help investors identify opportunities for growth and minimize risk. In this chapter, we will discuss in detail the key factors to consider when evaluating a property for multi-family real estate investing.

Physical Condition

The physical condition of the property is a critical factor to consider when evaluating a potential investment. This includes inspecting the building systems, such as electrical, plumbing, and HVAC systems, as well as the structural integrity of the property.

A comprehensive inspection of the property can help identify any issues or necessary repairs, such as outdated electrical systems or leaky roofs. These factors can impact the property's overall appeal to tenants and its ability to generate income. Additionally, investors should evaluate the condition of the common areas, such as hallways, stairwells, and parking lots, to ensure that they are well-maintained and can attract and retain tenants.

The age, location, and amenities of the property are also important physical factors to consider. Older properties may require more maintenance and repairs, while properties located in desirable areas with access to public transportation and other amenities may command higher rents. Investors should also consider the property's curb appeal, landscaping, and overall condition to determine its potential to attract tenants and generate income.

Financial Condition

The financial performance of the property is another critical factor to consider when evaluating a potential investment. This includes reviewing the property's income statement, balance sheet, and cash flow statement. Key financial metrics to consider include the net operating income (NOI), capitalization rate (cap rate), and cash-on-cash return.

The NOI represents the property's income minus its operating expenses, not including debt service. The cap rate is calculated by dividing the property's NOI by its value. The cash-on-cash return represents the annual cash flow generated by the property divided by the amount of equity invested.

Other important financial factors to consider include the property's debt service coverage ratio (DSCR) and vacancy rate. The DSCR measures the property's ability to cover its debt obligations, while the vacancy rate reflects the property's occupancy levels.

Investors should also evaluate the property's financing options, such as interest rates, terms of the loan, and any prepayment penalties. This can have a significant impact on the property's overall profitability and should be carefully considered when evaluating a potential investment.

The market analysis of the property involves evaluating the local rental market to determine the demand for rental units in the area, as well as the prevailing rental rates. This includes researching the local rental market to determine the demand for rental units in the area and the demographics of the local population.

Investors should also evaluate the supply and demand dynamics of the local rental market, as well as any regulatory or zoning issues that may impact the property's operations. Factors such as job growth, unemployment rates, and the availability of public transportation and other amenities can impact the property's ability to attract and retain tenants.

Evaluating the property is a critical step in multi-family real estate investing. The physical condition, financial performance, and market dynamics of the property should be carefully evaluated to determine its potential profitability and identify any risks or issues that may impact the investment. By conducting a comprehensive evaluation of the property, investors can make informed decisions and minimize their risk of financial loss. It is important to note that property evaluation is an ongoing process, and investors should regularly evaluate the property's performance and make adjustments as needed to maximize its profitability.

Assessing the condition of a multi-family property is a crucial step in real estate investing. It helps investors to evaluate the physical state of the property to identify any necessary repairs or improvements, as well as determine the overall appeal of the property to potential tenants. In this chapter, we will discuss in detail the key factors to consider when assessing the condition of a property for multi-family real estate investing.

The first area to assess when evaluating a multi-family property is the condition of the building systems. This includes inspecting the electrical, plumbing, and HVAC systems to ensure that they are in good working condition and do not pose any safety hazards to tenants. Any necessary repairs or upgrades should be factored into the overall cost of the property and assessed for their impact on the property's potential profitability.

The structural integrity of the building is another important factor to consider when assessing the condition of a multi-family property. A structural inspection can identify any potential issues, such as foundation problems or damage to the building's exterior. These issues can impact the safety of the property and should be addressed before investing in the property. Just because there is an issue, doesn't mean that the property isn't a good candidate for investment. Often times issues mean considerable discounts. Factor the cost of fixing these issues into your costs. If you factor in all of these costs on a property that has been discounted, you might find that the property will still cash flow. Make sure to account for all costs, short term and long term. Make sure the investment cash flows and meets your criteria.

Make sure everything gets inspected and documented. The condition of the common areas, such as hallways, stairwells, and parking lots, is an important consideration when assessing a multi-family property. These areas should be well-maintained and free from any safety hazards. Any necessary repairs or upgrades should be factored into the overall cost of the property.

Amenities, such as swimming pools or fitness centers, are also an important factor to consider when assessing the condition of a property. These amenities can attract and retain tenants, but they require ongoing maintenance and repairs. Investors should evaluate the costs associated with maintaining and repairing these amenities and assess their impact on the property's potential profitability.

The age of the property and its location are also important factors to consider when assessing its condition. Older properties may require more maintenance and repairs, while newer properties may have higher upfront costs but lower ongoing maintenance expenses. The property's location can impact its appeal to tenants, as properties located in desirable areas with access to public transportation and other amenities may command higher rents.

The curb appeal and overall condition of the property are important considerations when assessing its condition. The property should be well-maintained and free from any safety hazards, with attractive landscaping and well-maintained exterior features. A well-maintained property can attract and retain tenants, increasing its potential for profitability.

Investors should also evaluate the condition of the individual units within the property. This includes assessing the condition of the walls, floors, and ceilings, as well as the fixtures and appliances. Any necessary repairs or upgrades should be factored into the overall cost of the property and assessed for their impact on the property's potential profitability.

Assessing the condition of a multi-family property is a critical step in real estate investing. The physical state of the property, including the building systems, common areas, amenities, age, location, curb appeal, overall condition, and individual units should be carefully evaluated to identify any necessary repairs or improvements and assess the property's potential for profitability. By conducting a comprehensive assessment of the property's condition, investors can make informed decisions and minimize their risk of financial loss.

When evaluating a multi-family real estate investment, understanding the potential for improvements is critical to maximizing the property's profitability. Improvements can come in many forms, including renovations, upgrades to building systems and amenities, and changes to the property's management and operations. In this chapter, we will discuss in detail the key factors to consider when assessing the potential for improvements in a multi-family real estate investment.

The first step in assessing the potential for improvements is to evaluate the property's condition. This includes assessing the condition of the building systems, common areas, and individual units, as well as the property's age and location. Understanding the current state of the property can help identify areas for improvement and determine the associated costs and potential return on investment.

Renovations and upgrades can significantly improve the value of a multi-family property. For example, updating the building's exterior, landscaping, and common areas can increase its curb appeal and attract tenants. Upgrading the building systems, such as electrical, plumbing, and HVAC systems, can reduce maintenance costs and improve energy efficiency, leading to lower operating expenses and increased profitability.

Investors should also evaluate the condition of the individual units within the property. Upgrades to the individual units, such as updated fixtures, flooring, and appliances, can attract and retain tenants and increase the property's profitability.

The property's management and operations are also important factors to consider when assessing the potential for improvements. Effective management and operations can increase tenant satisfaction and retention, leading to higher occupancy rates and increased profitability.

Property managers should evaluate the property's current management and operations, including rent collection procedures, tenant screening processes, and maintenance procedures. By identifying areas for improvement and implementing effective management and operations strategies, investors can maximize the property's profitability.

Improvements to the property's management and operations can also include changes to the property's leasing strategies. Adjusting the lease terms or offering move-in specials can attract new tenants and increase occupancy rates.

Another important factor to consider when assessing the potential for improvements is the property's amenities and services. Upgrading or adding amenities, such as fitness centers, swimming pools, or community spaces, can attract and retain tenants and increase the property's profitability.

Additionally, providing services such as laundry facilities or on-site storage can add value to the property and generate additional income. Investors should evaluate the costs associated with adding or upgrading amenities and services and assess their potential impact on the property's profitability.

Investors should also conduct a market analysis to identify the amenities and services that are in high demand among renters in the area. This can help inform decisions about which amenities and services to add or upgrade to maximize the property's profitability.

Understanding the potential for improvements is a critical step in multi-family real estate investing. Renovations, upgrades to building systems and amenities, changes to management and operations, and the addition of amenities and services can significantly improve the value of a property and increase its profitability. By assessing the property's condition, management and operations, amenities and services, and conducting a market analysis, investors can identify areas for improvement and make informed decisions to maximize their return on investment.

CHAPTER FOUR

Leveraging

Leverage is a fundamental concept in finance and investing that involves using borrowed funds or financial instruments to magnify the potential returns of an investment. It can be a powerful tool that enhances profitability, but it also introduces additional risks. This chapter will explain the concept of leverage, its various forms, and its implications for us as investors.

What is Leverage? Leverage refers to the use of borrowed capital or financial instruments to increase the potential return on investment. It allows investors to control larger positions or assets with a smaller amount of their own capital.

Understanding Leverage

Leverage amplifies both gains and losses, intensifying the risk and potential reward of an investment. It can be employed in different forms, such as debt leverage, operational leverage, and financial derivatives.

There are different types of Leverage. For us as real estate investors, we are most concerned with debt leverage and operational leverage.

Debt leverage involves borrowing money to invest in assets or projects with the expectation of generating a return that exceeds the cost of borrowing. It commonly applies to real estate, corporate finance, and personal investments, using loans or bonds to finance acquisitions, expansions, or other ventures. For example, you can acquire and control a property by investing 20% of the value of the acquisition and borrowing the remaining 80%. You control the entire property and get the full benefit of that control even though you have only invested 20% of the value. For this example, you leveraged your investment of 20% to control 100% of the property. Another example of debt leverage, also relevant for us as real estate investors: You invest in amenities for the property you control because you know that the investment you make in the cost of adding those amenities will reduce your vacancy rate, increase your rents and the value of your property. The profits and increased the value of your property from adding these amenities will be greater than the cost of the investment in the amenities. In this example, you leveraged your investment in the amenities for increased income and value of your property.

Operational leverage pertains to the use of fixed costs in a business to amplify the impact of changes in sales or revenue on the company's profitability. It arises from having a high proportion of fixed costs relative to variable costs, which results in a higher degree of sensitivity to changes in income. For example, the fixed costs of a multi family property are the cost of the mortgage, property taxes, insurance, property management and maintenance. Relative costs might be from something like an increased cost in maintenance due to larger than anticipated repair.

What are the Benefits and Risks of Leverage?

Benefits of Leverage. Potential for higher returns. Leverage can amplify gains, allowing investors to generate larger profits than if they had solely used their own capital. Increased investment capacity. Leverage enables investors to control larger positions or assets, opening up opportunities that may have been otherwise inaccessible.

What are the Risks of Leverage?

One of the biggest risks of leverage is magnified losses. Just as leverage multiplies potential gains, it also intensifies losses. If the investment performs poorly, the losses will be larger than if no leverage had been employed.

Interest and financing costs associated with borrowing funds or utilizing financial derivatives come with associated costs in the form of interest payments and transactional fees at the time of financing.

Increased volatility by leveraging your investment can heighten the volatility of an investment portfolio, as it amplifies the impact of price fluctuations.

Considerations for Leveraged Investments

Proper risk assessment and management are crucial when using leverage. Investors should have a thorough understanding of the risks involved and establish appropriate risk mitigation strategies. As a real estate investor, your biggest risk in using leverage to acquire control of properties is defaulting on the loan for the property.

As real estate investors, using leverage increases your return on your investment. Lets use some basic numbers for this example. Lets say we can purchase properties in a certain market for about $50,000 each. These $50,000 properties can return about $6,000 each per year in profit. You have $100,000. With that $100,000, you can purchase two of these properties outright. Your annual profit on your $100,000 investment would be $12,000 or 12% If you use leverage, using your $100,000 to put 20% down payments on these $50,000 investment properties, you can now acquire and control 10 of these properties. Adjusting for the now added cost of mortgage payments, you are now making $5,000 profit on each of your properties every year. Your return on your $100,000 investment is now $50,000 a year, a 50% annual return on your investment. In this example, you leveraged your investment to not only increase your annual return on investment but to also increase your actual profit by more than 4 times if you hadn't used leverage and you acquired more assets and grew your portfolio by 5 times as many properties.

Leveraging is one of the most powerful investing strategies and one that I use for nearly every single one of my own investment's. Using leverage allows me to acquire and control a greater number of properties and also allows me a greater annual return on my investment.

CHAPTER FIVE

Financing Options

Multi-family real estate investing is a complex but lucrative field that can offer significant financial returns over the long-term. However, investing in multi-family properties can be an expensive proposition, and often requires significant financial resources. This is why it is important to carefully consider your financing options to ensure that you are able to secure the necessary funds to complete your investment.

Conventional Financing

Conventional Financing is one of the most common ways to finance multi-family real estate investing. This option involves obtaining a mortgage loan from a bank or other financial institution. Conventional loans can have fixed or variable interest rates, with repayment terms that typically range from 15 to 30 years. Conventional financing offers lower interest rates and longer repayment terms than other types of loans. The loan amount, interest rate, and repayment terms will depend on the borrowers creditworthiness, the value of the property, and other factors.

To qualify for conventional financing, you will need to have a good credit history and a strong financial standing. The bank or lender will examine your credit score, income, and other financial information to determine whether you are a good candidate for a loan. You will also need to provide a down payment, which typically ranges from 10% to 25% of the property's purchase price.

The loan amount you can qualify for will depend on several factors, including the value of the property, your creditworthiness, and the lender's underwriting standards. Interest rates for conventional loans are typically fixed or variable and can range from 3% to 6%, depending on the lender and your creditworthiness.

Repayment terms for conventional loans typically range from 15 to 30 years. The length of your repayment term will depend on the amount of the loan, the interest rate, and your financial circumstances. You will be required to make monthly payments, which will include principal and interest, until the loan is fully repaid.

The loan-to-value (LTV) ratio is the percentage of the property's value that the lender is willing to loan you. For conventional loans, the LTV ratio is typically between 70% and 80% of the property's appraised value. This means that you will need to provide a down payment of between 20% and 30% of the property's purchase price.

Government-backed loans, such as those offered by the Federal Housing Administration (FHA) and the Department of Veterans Affairs (VA), can be an attractive financing option for multi-family real estate investors and are considered conventional financing. These loans often have lower down payment requirements and more flexible qualification criteria than conventional loans. For example, FHA loans require a down payment of only 3.5% for multi-family properties, compared to the 20% typically required for conventional loans. VA loans do not require a down payment at all. In this chapter, we will provide more details on the different types of government-backed loans available for multi-family investments and their benefits and drawbacks.

FHA loans are backed by the Federal Housing Administration and are designed to help low-to-moderate income borrowers purchase homes, including multi-family properties. FHA loans require a down payment of only 3.5% for multi-family properties, compared to the 20% typically required for conventional loans. The maximum loan amount for an FHA loan varies depending on the location of the property and ranges from \$356,362 to \$822,375. Additionally, FHA loans have less strict credit score requirements than conventional loans, making them a popular option for investors who have less-than-perfect credit.

To qualify for an FHA loan, you will need to have a minimum credit score of 580 and a debt-to-income ratio of 43% or less. This means that your total debt payments cannot exceed 43% of your gross income. You will also need to provide a down payment of at least 3.5% of the property's purchase price. The property must be owner-occupied, meaning that at least one of the units must be occupied by the owner.

The maximum loan amount for an FHA loan varies depending on the location of the property and ranges from \$356,362 to \$822,375. This means that you can purchase multi-family properties with up to four units using an FHA loan. The loan limits for FHA loans are updated annually and are based on the median home prices in each area.

FHA loans have fixed interest rates and repayment terms that range from 15 to 30 years. The length of your repayment term will depend on the amount of the loan, the interest rate, and your financial circumstances. You will be required to make monthly payments, which will include principal and interest, until the loan is fully repaid.

One of the main benefits of FHA loans is that they require a lower down payment than conventional loans, which can be especially beneficial for multi-family investors who may not have a large amount of cash reserves. Additionally, FHA loans have less strict credit score requirements than conventional loans, making them a popular option for investors who have less-than-perfect credit. FHA loans also have lower interest rates than conventional loans, which can help to lower your monthly payments and improve your cash flow. Finally, FHA loans are assumable, which means that the buyer can take over the seller's existing mortgage under certain conditions, making the property more attractive to potential buyers.

One of the drawbacks of FHA loans is that they require mortgage insurance, which can increase the overall cost of the loan. The mortgage insurance is paid as an upfront fee at closing and as a monthly premium included in your monthly payments. Additionally, FHA loans often have stricter appraisal and inspection requirements than conventional loans, which can result in additional costs and may cause delays in the financing process. Finally, FHA loans are limited to owner-occupied properties, meaning that investors cannot use FHA loans to purchase properties that are solely for investment purposes.

When considering FHA loans for multi-family real estate investing, it is important to work with a qualified financial advisor and real estate attorney to ensure that you fully understand the terms and conditions of any loan agreement before signing on the dotted line. By understanding the qualifications, loan limits, repayment terms, benefits, and drawbacks of FHA loans, investors can make an informed decision about whether this type of financing is the right choice for their investment goals.

VA loans are backed by the Department of Veterans Affairs and are designed for active-duty military personnel, veterans, and their families. VA loans do not require a down payment, making them an attractive option for multi-family investors who want to conserve their cash reserves. Additionally, VA loans have less strict credit score requirements than conventional loans, and they often have lower interest rates. The loan limits for VA loans depend on the borrower's entitlement and the location of the property.

To qualify for a VA loan, you must be an active-duty military personnel, veteran, or the spouse of a military member who died while on active duty. You will need to provide a Certificate of Eligibility from the Department of Veterans Affairs to prove that you are eligible for a VA loan. To qualify for a VA loan, you will need to have a minimum credit score of 620 and a debt-to-income ratio of 41% or less.

The loan limits for VA loans depend on the borrower's entitlement and the location of the property. In most areas, the maximum loan amount for a VA loan is $548,250. However, in certain high-cost areas, the maximum loan amount can be as high as $822,375. The loan limits for VA loans are updated annually and are based on the median home prices in each area.

VA loans have fixed interest rates and repayment terms that range from 15 to 30 years. The length of your repayment term will depend on the amount of the loan, the interest rate, and your financial circumstances. You will be required to make monthly payments, which will include principal and interest, until the loan is fully repaid.

One of the main benefits of VA loans is that they do not require a down payment, which can be especially beneficial for multi-family investors who want to conserve their cash reserves. Additionally, VA loans have less strict credit score requirements than conventional loans, making them a popular option for investors who have less-than-perfect credit. VA loans also often have lower interest rates than conventional loans, which can help to lower your monthly payments and improve your cash flow. Finally, VA loans are assumable, which means that the buyer can take over the seller's existing mortgage under certain conditions, making the property more attractive to potential buyers.

One of the drawbacks of VA loans is that they require a funding fee, which can increase the overall cost of the loan. The funding fee varies depending on the type of loan, the amount of the down payment, and the borrower's military service status. Additionally, VA loans often have stricter appraisal and inspection requirements than conventional loans, which can result in additional costs and may cause delays in the financing process.

When considering VA loans for multi-family real estate investing, it is important to work with a qualified financial advisor and real estate attorney to ensure that you fully understand the terms and conditions of any loan agreement before signing on the dotted line. By understanding the qualifications, loan limits, repayment terms, benefits, and drawbacks of VA loans, investors can make an informed decision about whether this type of financing is the right choice for their investment goals.

USDA loans are backed by the United States Department of Agriculture and are designed to help rural residents purchase homes and multi-family properties. These loans require no down payment and have lower interest rates than conventional loans. However, USDA loans are limited to certain geographic areas and income levels. Additionally, borrowers must meet certain eligibility requirements, including income limits and creditworthiness.

Qualifying for USDA Loans: To qualify for a USDA loan, the property must be located in a rural area as designated by the United States Department of Agriculture. The borrower must also meet income eligibility requirements, which vary depending on the location of the property and the size of the borrower's household. Additionally, the borrower will need to have a minimum credit score of 640 and a debt-to-income ratio of 41% or less. It's important to note that the USDA loan program is only available for owner-occupied properties.

The loan limits for USDA loans depend on the location of the property and the number of units in the multi-family property. In general, the maximum loan amount for a USDA loan is $1,118,550 for properties with up to four units. However, the loan limits for USDA loans are subject to change each year and vary depending on the median home prices in each area.

USDA loans have fixed interest rates and repayment terms that range from 15 to 30 years. The length of your repayment term will depend on the amount of the loan, the interest rate, and your financial circumstances. You will be required to make monthly payments, which will include principal and interest, until the loan is fully repaid.

One of the main benefits of USDA loans is that they offer low interest rates, which can help to lower your monthly payments and improve your cash flow. Additionally, USDA loans do not require a down payment, which can be especially beneficial for multi-family investors who want to conserve their cash reserves. USDA loans also have less strict credit score requirements than conventional loans, making them a popular option for investors who have less-than-perfect credit. Finally, USDA loans often have longer repayment terms than conventional loans, which can help to lower your monthly payments and improve your cash flow.

One of the drawbacks of USDA loans is that the property must be located in a rural area, which can limit the pool of potential properties to invest in. Additionally, USDA loans often have stricter appraisal and inspection requirements than conventional loans, which can result in additional costs and may cause delays in the financing process. Finally, the USDA loan program is only available for owner-occupied properties, which means that it cannot be used for purely investment purposes.

When considering USDA loans for multi-family real estate investing, it is important to work with a qualified financial advisor and real estate attorney to ensure that you fully understand the terms and conditions of any loan agreement before signing on the dotted line. By understanding the qualifications, loan limits, repayment terms, benefits, and drawbacks of USDA loans, investors can make an informed decision about whether this type of financing is the right choice for their investment goals.

One of the benefits of government-backed loans is that they typically have lower down payment requirements than conventional loans, making them more accessible to a wider range of investors. They also often have more flexible qualification criteria, which can make it easier for investors to obtain financing. Additionally, government-backed loans often have lower interest rates than conventional loans, which can help to lower your monthly payments and improve your cash flow.

One of the drawbacks of government-backed loans is that they often have stricter appraisal and inspection requirements than conventional loans. This can result in additional costs and may cause delays in the financing process. Additionally, some government-backed loans require mortgage insurance, which can increase the overall cost of the loan. Finally, government-backed loans often have more paperwork and a longer application process than conventional loans, which can be a barrier to entry for some investors.

When considering government-backed loans for multi-family real estate investing, it is important to work with a qualified financial advisor and real estate attorney to ensure that you fully understand the terms and conditions of any loan agreement before signing on the dotted line. By understanding the details of FHA, VA, and USDA loans, investors can make an informed decision about whether government-backed loans are the right choice for their investment goals.

One of the benefits of conventional financing is that it is widely available and offered by many financial institutions. This makes it a convenient option for investors who have a good credit history and a strong financial standing. Additionally, conventional financing offers longer repayment terms than some other types of loans, which can help to lower your monthly payments and improve your cash flow.

However, one of the drawbacks of conventional financing is that it typically requires a significant down payment, which can be a barrier to entry for some investors. Additionally, conventional loans often require more paperwork and a longer application process than other types of loans. Finally, if you have a lower credit score or a high debt-to-income ratio, you may not qualify for a conventional loan or may be offered less favorable terms.

When considering conventional financing for multi-family real estate investing, it is important to work with a qualified financial advisor and real estate attorney to ensure that you fully understand the terms and conditions of any loan agreement before signing on the dotted line. By understanding the qualifications, loan amounts, interest rates, repayment terms, and loan-to-value ratio, you can make an informed decision about whether conventional financing is the right choice for your investment goals.

Hard Money Loans

Hard money loans are short-term loans that are typically used by real estate investors to finance the purchase and renovation of properties. These loans are often easier to qualify for than conventional loans, but they come with higher interest rates and fees. Hard money lenders are typically private individuals or companies who are willing to lend money based on the value of the property rather than the borrower's creditworthiness.

Qualifying for Hard Money Loans: The primary qualification for a hard money loan is the value of the property being purchased. Unlike traditional lending sources, hard money lenders are less concerned with the borrower's credit score or financial history, and are primarily focused on the property's value and potential for generating income. However, hard money lenders often require a significant down payment or equity in the property to reduce their risk.

Hard money loans typically have higher interest rates and shorter repayment terms than other types of loans. The loan limits for hard money loans vary depending on the lender and the property being financed, but generally, they can range from a few hundred thousand dollars to several million dollars. The loan-to-value ratio for hard money loans may be lower than other types of loans, which means that the borrower may need to provide more equity in the property.

Hard money loans have short repayment terms, typically ranging from six months to three years. This means that the borrower must be able to repay the loan within a relatively short period, usually by refinancing the property or selling it. Hard money loans often have balloon payments, which require the borrower to pay off the entire loan balance at the end of the repayment term.

One of the main benefits of hard money loans is that they offer fast funding, which can be especially useful for multi-family real estate investors who need to move quickly to secure a property. Hard money loans also often have flexible qualification criteria, which means that borrowers who may not qualify for other types of loans may still be able to secure funding. Additionally, hard money loans often have a high degree of flexibility, which allows the borrower to negotiate repayment terms and other loan conditions to better suit their needs.

One of the main drawbacks of hard money loans is that they have higher interest rates and shorter repayment terms than other types of loans. This can make them more expensive in the long run, especially if the borrower is unable to repay the loan within the repayment term. Additionally, hard money loans often have higher fees and costs associated with them, such as appraisal fees, origination fees, and closing costs. Finally, hard money lenders may be less transparent in their lending practices, which can lead to misunderstandings or disputes down the line.

When considering hard money loans for multi-family real estate investing, it is important to work with a qualified financial advisor and real estate attorney to ensure that you fully understand the terms and conditions of any loan agreement before signing on the dotted line. By understanding the qualifications, loan limits, repayment terms, benefits, and drawbacks of hard money loans, investors can make an informed decision about whether this type of financing is the right choice for their investment goals.

Private Financing

Private financing also known as private money is another option for multi-family real estate investors. This can involve borrowing money from friends or family members or working with private lenders who specialize in real estate investing. Private financing can be a good option for investors who have difficulty obtaining financing through traditional channels, or who want to avoid the strict qualification criteria of conventional loans.

Qualifying for Private Financing: Qualifying for private financing is typically easier than qualifying for traditional financing options, as private lenders are often more flexible in their qualification criteria. Private lenders may take into account factors such as the borrower's experience in real estate investing, the potential for income from the property, and the borrower's overall financial situation. However, private lenders may also require a higher down payment or equity in the property to mitigate their risk.

Private financing is often more flexible in terms of loan limits than traditional financing options, as private lenders may be willing to provide financing for larger amounts than traditional lenders. However, the loan limits for private financing will depend on the individual lender and the property being financed.

Private financing typically has shorter repayment terms than traditional financing options, often ranging from one to five years. This means that the borrower must be able to repay the loan within a relatively short period, usually by refinancing the property or selling it. Private lenders may also require balloon payments, which require the borrower to pay off the entire loan balance at the end of the repayment term.

One of the main benefits of private financing is that it offers more flexibility than traditional financing options. Private lenders are often willing to negotiate repayment terms and other loan conditions to better suit the needs of the borrower. Additionally, private financing can be a good option for multi-family real estate investors who have less-than-perfect credit or who are unable to obtain financing through traditional channels. Private financing also often offers fast funding, which can be especially useful for investors who need to move quickly to secure a property.

One of the main drawbacks of private financing is that it often comes with higher interest rates and fees than traditional financing options. Private lenders may also require a higher down payment or equity in the property to mitigate their risk. Additionally, private financing is often less regulated than traditional financing options, which can lead to misunderstandings or disputes down the line.

When considering private financing for multi-family real estate investments, it is important to work with a qualified financial advisor and real estate attorney to ensure that you fully understand the terms and conditions of any loan agreement before signing on the dotted line. By understanding the qualifications, loan limits, repayment terms, benefits, and drawbacks of private financing, investors can make an informed decision about whether this type of financing is the right choice for their investment goals.

Syndication Financing

Syndication is a popular way for real estate investors to pool their resources and invest in larger properties. In a syndication, a group of investors contribute capital to purchase and operate a multi-family property. The investors share in the profits and expenses according to their ownership percentages. Syndication can be a good option for investors who want to spread their risk across multiple investors and properties.

How Syndication Financing Works: Syndication financing involves a group of investors pooling their money together to purchase a multi-family property. The investors form a Limited Liability Company (LLC) or Limited Partnership (LP) to oversee the investment and provide legal protection for the investors. The LLC or LP then borrows the necessary funds from a lender to purchase the property. The investors typically receive a return on their investment through the property's cash flow, as well as through appreciation in the property's value.

Qualifying for syndication financing typically requires a strong investment plan and a proven track record in real estate investing. Investors will want to see a well-researched and well-developed business plan that includes projections for the property's income and expenses. Additionally, the investor group will need to have a solid credit history and financial background to secure financing. Syndication financing can also benefit from having a diverse group of investors, each with their own expertise and skills to contribute to the project.

The loan limits for syndication financing will depend on the size of the investment group and the property being financed. In general, syndication financing can provide access to larger amounts of capital than individual investors would be able to obtain on their own. This can be especially beneficial for multi-family real estate investors who are looking to purchase larger properties that require significant capital investments.

Syndication financing typically has longer repayment terms than other types of financing options, often ranging from five to ten years. This means that the investors have a longer period to repay the loan and receive a return on their investment. Additionally, the repayment terms for syndication financing can often be negotiated to better suit the needs of the investors and the investment project. However, syndication financing may also come with higher interest rates and fees than other types of financing options.

One of the main benefits of syndication financing is that it allows investors to pool their resources to purchase larger properties than they could on their own. Additionally, syndication financing allows for greater flexibility in financing options and repayment terms. Syndication financing also offers the potential for higher returns on investment than other types of financing options, as the investors can benefit from economies of scale and the ability to purchase a larger property with a larger potential for income and appreciation.

One of the main drawbacks of syndication financing is that it requires a significant amount of time and effort to develop and implement a well-researched business plan that will appeal to potential investors. Additionally, syndication financing may come with higher fees and costs associated with forming the LLC or LP and securing financing. Syndication financing also requires a significant amount of coordination and communication among the investors and the project team, which can be challenging to manage.

Syndication financing can be an attractive financing option for multi-family real estate investors who are looking to purchase larger properties or who need to raise more capital than they can on their own. By understanding the qualifications, loan limits, repayment terms, benefits, and drawbacks of syndication financing, investors can make an informed decision about whether this type of financing is the right choice for their investment goals. It is important to work with a qualified financial advisor and real estate attorney to ensure that you fully understand the terms and conditions of any investment or financing agreement before signing on the dotted line.

Seller Financing

Seller financing is a creative way to finance a multi-family property and is one of my favorites whenever I can make it happen. Understand though that this is not as common as we investors would like it to be. With this option, the seller of the property agrees to finance part or all of the purchase price. This can be a good option for investors who have difficulty obtaining financing through traditional channels, or who want to avoid the strict qualification criteria of conventional loans. Seller financing can also be a good option for sellers who are motivated to sell quickly, as it can help them avoid the time and expense of listing their property on the open market.

Seller financing involves the seller of a property providing a loan to the buyer for the purchase of the property. The terms of the loan are negotiated between the buyer and the seller, and typically include a down payment, interest rate, repayment term, and other loan conditions. The buyer then makes payments to the seller over the course of the loan term until the loan is fully repaid. The loan is secured by the property, and the seller retains a lien on the property until the loan is fully repaid.

Qualifying for seller financing is typically easier than qualifying for traditional financing options, as the seller is often more flexible in their qualification criteria. However, the seller may require a larger down payment or equity in the property to mitigate their risk. The seller may also require proof of the buyer's financial stability and creditworthiness. It is important for the buyer to have a clear understanding of the seller's requirements and to provide all necessary documentation and information to support their application for seller financing.

The loan limits for seller financing will depend on the individual seller and the property being financed. However, seller financing can provide access to larger amounts of capital than traditional financing options, as the seller may be willing to provide financing for the full purchase price of the property. The loan amount will also depend on the buyer's ability to make the required payments and the overall value of the property.

Seller financing typically has shorter repayment terms than traditional financing options, often ranging from one to ten years. This means that the buyer must be able to repay the loan within a relatively short period, usually by refinancing the property or selling it. Seller financing may also come with balloon payments, which require the buyer to pay off the entire loan balance at the end of the repayment term. It is important for the buyer to carefully review the loan terms and to ensure that they have a clear plan for repaying the loan within the required time frame.

One of the main benefits of seller financing is that it allows multi-family real estate investors to bypass the strict qualification criteria and requirements of traditional lenders. Seller financing can also be a good option for investors who have less-than-perfect credit or who are unable to obtain financing through traditional channels. Additionally, seller financing often offers fast funding, which can be especially useful for investors who need to move quickly to secure a property. Seller financing can also offer greater flexibility in loan terms and repayment options, as the terms of the loan are negotiated directly between the buyer and the seller.

One of the main drawbacks of seller financing is that it often comes with higher interest rates and fees than traditional financing options.

Additionally, seller financing may require a larger down payment or equity in the property to mitigate the seller's risk. The seller may also retain a lien on the property until the loan is fully repaid, which can limit the buyer's ability to make changes or improvements to the property. It is important for the buyer to carefully review the loan terms and to ensure that they fully understand the interest rates, fees, and other loan conditions.

Seller financing can be an attractive financing option for multi-family real estate investors who are unable to obtain financing through traditional channels or who want more flexibility in their loan terms. By understanding the qualifications, loan limits, repayment terms, benefits, and drawbacks of seller financing, investors can make an informed decision about whether this type of financing is the right choice for their investment goals.

Crowdfunding

Crowdfunding is a newer financing option that allows investors to pool their funds online to invest in multi-family properties. Crowdfunding platforms typically charge a fee for their services and require a minimum investment amount. Crowdfunding is a good option for smaller investors who want to invest in real estate but do not have access to large amounts of capital.

Crowdfunding platforms for multi-family investment purchases typically require a minimum investment amount, which can range from a few hundred dollars to tens of thousands of dollars. The platform also charges a fee for their services, typically a percentage of the total amount raised.

Investors who choose to invest in multi-family properties through crowdfunding platforms have several benefits. One of the main benefits is the ability to invest in larger real estate projects without needing to come up with the entire investment amount on their own. This makes investing in multi-family properties more accessible to a broader range of investors.

Another benefit of crowdfunding for multi-family investment purchases is the ease of investing. Crowdfunding platforms make it easy for investors to browse and invest in properties from anywhere with an internet connection. Additionally, investors don't have to deal with the day-to-day management of the property, as this is typically handled by the property management company.

Investing in multi-family properties through crowdfunding also allows for a more diverse portfolio, as investors can spread their funds across multiple properties, reducing their risk exposure. Crowdfunding platforms also provide investors with access to a wider range of investment opportunities, including properties in different locations, asset classes, and risk profiles.

However, investing in multi-family properties through crowdfunding does have some drawbacks. One of the main drawbacks is the lack of control over the investment. Investors do not have direct control over the property, and their ability to make decisions about the property may be limited. Additionally, investors may have limited access to information about the property and may have to rely on the crowdfunding platform to provide updates.

Another drawback of crowdfunding for multi-family investment purchases is the potential for lower returns compared to direct ownership. Crowdfunding platforms charge fees for their services, which can reduce the overall return on investment. Additionally, investors may have to share the rental income with other investors, further reducing their returns.

Crowdfunding for multi-family investment purchases can be a viable financing option for investors who are looking to diversify their real estate portfolio and invest in larger projects. Crowdfunding allows investors to pool their funds together and invest in properties that may have otherwise been out of reach. However, investors should carefully evaluate the risks and benefits of crowdfunding before investing, as there are potential drawbacks to this financing option, such as limited control over the investment and lower returns due to platform fees. As with any real estate investment, working with a trusted advisor or financial professional can help investors make informed decisions.

When evaluating your financing options, it is important to consider your overall financial goals and your risk tolerance. Each financing option comes with its own advantages and disadvantages, and it is important to carefully evaluate each option to determine which one is best suited to your needs. Additionally, it is important to work with a qualified real estate attorney and financial advisor to ensure that you fully understand the terms and conditions of any financing agreement before signing on the dotted line.

Interest rates and loan terms are two of the most important factors that affect the overall cost of financing for a real estate investment. Understanding these concepts is crucial for making informed decisions when financing a real estate investment.

Interest Rates

Interest rates are the cost of borrowing money for a real estate investment. The interest rate for a real estate investment can be fixed or variable. Fixed interest rates remain the same throughout the life of the loan, providing stability and predictability in monthly payments. Variable interest rates, on the other hand, can change over time, and provide more flexibility if interest rates decrease.

Interest rates are determined by a variety of factors, including the current state of the economy, inflation rates, and the perceived risk associated with the investment. Higher perceived risk generally results in higher interest rates, while lower perceived risk typically results in lower interest rates.

Interest rates are expressed as an annual percentage rate (APR). The APR takes into account the interest rate, any fees associated with the loan, and the loan term. The APR provides a more accurate representation of the overall cost of financing than the interest rate alone.

Loan Terms

Loan terms refer to the length of time over which the loan will be repaid. Loan terms can range from a few months to several decades, depending on the type of loan and the amount borrowed. Longer loan terms may result in lower monthly payments, but they also result in paying more interest over the life of the loan. Shorter loan terms may result in higher monthly payments, but they also result in paying less interest over the life of the loan.

Loan terms can also impact the investor's ability to sell the property. Loans with prepayment penalties can make it more challenging to sell the property before the loan term ends, as the penalties can be costly.

When evaluating financing options for a real estate investment, it's essential to consider both the interest rate and loan terms. Investors should evaluate the costs associated with each option, including interest rates, fees, and the loan term. They should also consider their overall investment strategy and goals, as well as their ability to make monthly payments and repay the loan.

Working with a trusted financial advisor or real estate agent can help investors navigate the complex financing process and make informed decisions. It's also important to monitor interest rates and loan terms over time, as they can change and impact the overall cost of financing for a real estate investment. Understanding interest rates and loan terms is crucial for making informed decisions when financing a real estate investment.

CHAPTER SIX

Conventional Financing

Conventional real estate financing refers to traditional methods of obtaining funding for the purchase or refinancing of real property Most investors use conventional financing to acquire their properties and conventional financing lends itself well to the use of leverage. In chapter 3 we covered many of the different types of conventional financing. This chapter covers the key aspects of conventional real estate financing, including loan types, eligibility requirements, application process, and considerations for borrowers.

Types of Conventional Real Estate Loans

The most common type of conventional real estate loan is a conventional mortgage, which is offered by banks, credit unions, and mortgage lenders. Conventional mortgages typically have fixed or adjustable interest rates and require a down payment, usually ranging from 3% to 20% of the property's purchase price.

Conforming Loans

Conforming loans are conventional mortgages that adhere to the guidelines set by government-sponsored enterprises (GSEs) like Fannie Mae and Freddie Mac. These loans must meet specific loan limits, borrower qualifications, and property requirements established by the GSEs.

Non-Conforming Loans

Non-conforming loans, also known as jumbo loans, exceed the loan limits set by the GSEs. Jumbo loans are often used for high-value properties and typically require larger down payments and stricter eligibility criteria.

Eligibility and Qualifications

As you no doubt already know, credit score and credit history are key factors in determining a borrowers eligibility for funding. Lenders consider the borrower's credit score and credit history to assess their creditworthiness. A higher credit score generally improves the borrower's chances of obtaining favorable loan terms.

Lenders also consider the borrowers income and employment. Borrowers must demonstrate a stable and sufficient income to repay the loan. Lenders typically verify employment history, income stability, and debt-to-income ratio to assess the borrower's ability to make timely mortgage payments. Most lenders will consider the potential income from an investment property as part of your income profile and factor this additional income into your ability to pay the loan.

In chapter four we discussed leverage. The most common type of leverage for us as investors is our down payment. Conventional loans require a down payment, usually ranging from 3% to 20% of the property's purchase price. The down payment amount can affect the loan terms and the need for private mortgage insurance (PMI).

Lenders consider the borrowers debt-to-income ratio. Lenders evaluate the borrower's debt-to-income ratio, comparing their monthly debt obligations to their income. A lower ratio indicates a healthier financial position and enhances the borrower's loan eligibility.

Application and Approval Process

If you want to have an idea of what type of loan, amounts, terms and considerations of that loan that you might qualify for before going out in search of your investment property, you can go to your lender and get prequalified for a loan. Borrowers can seek Prequalification to determine their borrowing capacity.

Prequalification involves a preliminary assessment of the borrower's financial situation based on information provided by the borrower.

Once you have determined the property that you are interested in acquiring using a conventional loan, you will start your mortgage application. The mortgage application process involves submitting detailed financial information, such as your income statements, tax returns, bank statements, and employment verification. Borrowers must complete an application form, disclose the property details, and pay applicable fees, including an application fee and appraisal fee.

After you complete your mortgage application, it goes to what is called Underwriting and Loan Approval. The lender's underwriting team assesses the borrower's application, verifies the provided information, and evaluates the property's value. They analyze creditworthiness, income stability, and compliance with lending guidelines. If approved, the lender issues a loan commitment letter outlining the terms and conditions of the approved loan.

Considerations for Borrowers

One of the factors that certainly deserves consideration but doesn't necessarily dictate whether or not you can profit from a property are interest rates and loan terms. Borrowers should compare interest rates, loan terms, and closing costs offered by different lenders to secure the most favorable financing option. Fixed-rate mortgages provide stability, while adjustable-rate mortgages (ARMs) offer initial lower rates that may adjust periodically.

Depending upon your loan terms and certainly your down payment amount, you may be required by the lender to pay Private Mortgage Insurance (PMI). Borrowers with a down payment less than 20% of the purchase price may be required to pay PMI, which protects the lender in case of default. Understanding the cost, duration, and conditions for PMI is essential for borrowers considering conventional loans with lower down payments.

At the end of all of this, you have to consider closing costs. Borrowers should anticipate closing costs, including appraisal fees, origination fees, title insurance, attorney fees, and prepaid property taxes and insurance. Comparing these costs among lenders can help borrowers minimize expenses.

Conventional real estate financing provides borrowers with a traditional and widely accessible means of purchasing or refinancing properties. Understanding the various loan types, eligibility requirements, application process, and associated considerations empowers borrowers to make informed decisions and secure financing that aligns with their financial goals and circumstances.

CHAPTER SEVEN

Hard Money

Hard money loans are a specialized form of real estate financing that offers borrowers an alternative source of funding when traditional lending options may be limited or unavailable. I often use hard money loans for certain situations when purchasing multi-family properties. It is a strategy that I use to purchase properties that need rehab or properties that I plan to quickly flip or refinance. Unlike conventional loans where the primary focus in on the eligibility of the borrower, hard money loans focus primarily on the value of the property being used as collateral, making them accessible to borrowers with unique circumstances or those who may not meet the stringent requirements of traditional lenders. This chapter covers the key aspects of hard money loans, including their definition, characteristics, advantages, considerations, and the application process.

Understanding Hard Money Loans

Hard money loans are short-term, asset-based loans and primarily used in real estate transactions. They are typically funded by private investors or specialized lending firms, rather than traditional financial institutions. The loan amount is determined by the value of the property being used as collateral, with less emphasis on the borrower's creditworthiness or income.

Hard money loans have characteristics that you won't find in conventional financing. Many of these characteristics are what makes Hard Money loans a better option at some times than conventional loans. Hard money loans possess several distinct characteristics that set them apart from traditional financing options. Hard money loans have shorter terms, often ranging from six months to a few years. This is because they are designed for short-term financing needs, such as property rehabilitation, acquisition, or flipping.

Due to the increased risk involved, hard money loans typically come with higher interest rates compared to conventional loans. The rates can vary depending on factors such as the loan-to-value ratio, the borrower's experience, and the property's condition.

Hard money loans are known for their expedited approval and funding processes. Unlike traditional loans that may take months to close, hard money loans can be approved and funded within days or weeks, providing borrowers with the opportunity to seize time-sensitive deals and investment opportunities.

Hard money loans are secured by the property itself, which serves as collateral. The value of the property is a critical factor in determining the loan amount, and lenders may conduct appraisals and property inspections to assess its condition and market value.

While creditworthiness and income are still considered, hard money lenders primarily focus on the value of the property and the borrower's equity. This flexibility makes hard money loans accessible to borrowers with less-than-perfect credit, self-employed individuals, and those who may not meet the stringent requirements of traditional lenders.

Advantages of Hard Money Loans

The expedited approval and funding processes associated with hard money loans offer significant advantages for borrowers.

In situations where time is of the essence, such as foreclosure auctions or competitive bidding scenarios, the quick approval and funding of hard money loans enable borrowers to secure properties and complete transactions promptly.

Hard money loans allow investors to capitalize on time-sensitive investment opportunities, such as acquiring properties at discounted prices or funding renovations and improvements to increase their value.

The flexible qualification criteria of hard money loans provide borrowers with additional advantages.

Borrowers with less-than-ideal credit scores or past financial difficulties can still access funding through hard money loans. Since the loan amount primarily relies on the property's value, creditworthiness plays a lesser role in the approval process.

Self-employed individuals who may face challenges in documenting their income or meeting the strict requirements of traditional lenders can benefit from the asset-based approach of hard money loans.

Hard money loans can be used for various property types, making them versatile financing options:

Hard money loans can be utilized for purchasing or refinancing residential properties, including single-family homes, townhouses, and condominiums.

Hard money loans are applicable to commercial real estate transactions, such as acquiring office buildings, retail spaces, or industrial properties.

Hard money loans are commonly employed in financing investment properties, including rental properties, multi-unit buildings, and fix-and-flip projects.

Hard money loans cater to borrowers facing specific circumstances.

Borrowers who have experienced foreclosure or bankruptcy may have difficulty obtaining traditional loans. Hard money lenders focus more on the value of the property and the borrower's equity, making these loans accessible in such situations.

Properties with unconventional characteristics or limited market appeal may face challenges in securing traditional financing. Hard money loans can provide funding for properties that do not meet the criteria of traditional lenders.

Considerations for Borrowers

Hard money loans come with higher interest rates and costs. Borrowers must carefully assess the costs associated with hard money loans, as they typically come with higher interest rates and fees compared to traditional loans. It is important to evaluate the potential returns on the investment and ensure that the project's profitability can cover the loan expenses.

The shorter terms of hard money loans necessitate careful financial planning.

Borrowers must develop a clear repayment strategy to ensure the loan can be repaid within the designated term. This may involve selling the property, refinancing with a traditional lender, or utilizing other sources of capital.

Knowing your exit strategy when using a hard money loan is essential. Hard money lenders typically expect borrowers to have a well-defined exit strategy, outlining how the loan will be repaid. Demonstrating a viable exit strategy strengthens the borrower's position when applying for a hard money loan.

Conducting thorough due diligence on the property is essential to mitigate risks.

It is advisable to obtain professional appraisals and inspections to accurately assess the property's condition, market value, and potential for appreciation.

Analyzing the local real estate market, including factors such as supply and demand, rental rates, and comparable property sales, helps determine the property's investment potential.

Selecting reputable and experienced hard money lenders is crucial.

Conduct your own research and due diligence on lenders and identify a few that you are comfortable working with. Borrowers should research and evaluate different hard money lenders, considering factors such as their track record, reputation, loan terms, and customer reviews.

Make sure the the lender you choose has open and transparent communication. Open and transparent communication with the lender is essential to ensure a clear understanding of the loan terms, repayment obligations, and potential risks.

The Hard Money Loan Application Process

We've already established that borrowers should conduct comprehensive research and analysis before applying for a hard money loan. Through this research, you should have identified the lenders you are interested in working with. Identify reputable hard money lenders who specialize in the desired property type and loan requirements. Understand the specific loan requirements, such as loan-to-value ratios, down payment expectations, and associated fees. Though many of the basics are the same, each hard money lender has their own specific application requirements. Understand what these are and make sure that you can meet these requirements.

The application process typically involves the following steps the lenders specific steps.

Prepare the necessary documentation, including the property's information, financial statements, and personal identification.

Create a loan proposal outlining the project's details, including the property's purchase price, scope of work, and expected timeline.

Submit the application and all required documents to the selected hard money lender.

The lender will conduct due diligence to assess the loan's viability. The lender may order an appraisal, property inspection, or title search to verify the property's value, condition, and marketability.

The lender will evaluate the borrower's financial capacity, including credit history, income, and previous real estate experience. If the loan application is approved, the lender will issue a loan commitment and proceed with funding.

The lender will outline the loan terms, interest rate, repayment schedule, and any additional conditions.

The borrower and lender will work together to complete the necessary closing documentation, including promissory notes, deeds of trust, and loan agreements. Once all closing requirements are met, the funds will be disbursed to the borrower.

Hard money loans offer a valuable financing option for real estate investors and borrowers who require quick funding, have unique circumstances, or cannot obtain traditional bank loans. Understanding the characteristics, advantages, considerations, and application process of hard money loans allows borrowers to make informed decisions and leverage this alternative funding source effectively in their real estate endeavors.

CHAPTER EIGHT

Private Money

So what do you do if you don't want to or don't qualify for a conventional or hard money loan? You go after "Private Money". Private money, also known as private lending or private financing, is a form of real estate investment funding provided by private individuals or groups. This is one of my favorite forms of financing investment properties and mastering this strategy will provide you with nearly unlimited funding with little to know personal impact. This chapter covers the key aspects of private money for real estate investment, including its definition, advantages, considerations, and how to secure private funding. We will delve into the intricacies of private money loans, including the characteristics, sources, due diligence, loan structuring, and the application process.

Understanding Private Money

Private money refers to funds provided by private individuals or groups, commonly referred to as private lenders or investors, for real estate investment purposes. These private lenders can include family members, friends, acquaintances, or professional private lending firms and my favorites, hedge funds and purpose built funds.

Private money loans possess distinct characteristics that set them apart from traditional financing options.

Private money loans often originate from personal relationships or connections between the borrower and the lender. This relationship-based approach allows for more flexible terms, personalized agreements, and customized repayment structures.

For the most part, private money loans are asset-based. Similar to hard money loans, private money loans are typically secured by the property being financed. The property serves as the collateral for the loan, reducing the emphasis on the borrower's creditworthiness and income.

Private money loans generally come with higher interest rates compared to conventional loans. This is due to the increased risk taken by private lenders who are providing funds based on the property's value and the borrower's investment strategy.

Private money loans typically have shorter terms, ranging from a few months to a few years. These loans are designed to provide short-term financing for real estate investment projects.

Advantages of Private Money

One of the greatest advantages of private money and the primary reason I love private money is the flexibility and speed associated with funding investment projects.. Private money loans offer several advantages for real estate investors. Because private money offers quick approval and funding, private money lenders often have streamlined approval processes, allowing for faster funding compared to traditional lenders. This enables investors to capitalize on time-sensitive opportunities and secure properties swiftly.

Private lenders have more flexibility in structuring loan terms. This can include customized repayment schedules, interest rates, and repayment options tailored to the specific needs of the borrower and the investment project.

Private money loans provide an alternative financing option for borrowers who may not meet the strict criteria of traditional lenders, such as those with less-than-perfect credit, self-employed individuals, or those looking to fund unique investment projects.

Private money loans are primarily based on the value of the property being used as collateral. This asset-based approach allows investors to secure funding based on the property's potential and value, rather than relying solely on their creditworthiness or income.

Private money lenders may be more open to financing unconventional or unique real estate investment projects. This can include properties with specific challenges or opportunities that traditional lenders may shy away from, providing investors with the ability to pursue creative and potentially lucrative deals.

In some cases, private money lenders may offer equity participation in the investment project. This means that instead of or in addition to charging interest, the lender receives a share of the profits when the property is sold or refinanced. This can align the interests of the lender and the borrower, fostering a mutually beneficial partnership.

Considerations for Borrowers

Building strong relationships with private lenders is crucial for securing private money loans. Networking and Referrals: Engaging in real estate investment networks, attending industry events, and seeking referrals from trusted contacts can help identify potential private lenders. Building a network of investors, professionals, and mentors in the real estate industry can provide access to reliable private money sources.

Developing trust and maintaining open communication with private lenders is essential. This includes providing detailed project plans, financial projections, and a clear strategy for loan repayment. Sharing accurate and transparent information builds credibility and instills confidence in the lender.

When considering private money loans, borrowers should conduct thorough due diligence on potential lenders. Research the track record, experience, and reputation of the private lender or lending firm. This includes reviewing past deals, client testimonials, and online reviews. Seek feedback from other borrowers who have worked with the lender to assess their experience and reliability. Ensure the private lender operates within legal and regulatory frameworks governing private lending activities in the relevant jurisdiction. Consult with legal professionals to ensure compliance with local laws and regulations.

Working with an attorney or experienced professionals in real estate finance is recommended to ensure proper loan structuring and documentation. Drafting a comprehensive loan agreement is essential to protect the interests of both the borrower and the lender. The loan agreement should outline the terms, interest rates, repayment schedule, default provisions, and any other relevant clauses.

Establishing appropriate security instruments, such as promissory notes, deeds of trust, or mortgage agreements, is crucial to secure the lender's interests and the property as collateral. These instruments should be properly executed and recorded as per local laws.

The Private Money Loan Application Process

Your private money loan application will include a loan proposal and presentation. When seeking private money loans, borrowers should prepare a compelling loan proposal and presentation. Clearly outline the investment project, including property information, market analysis, financial projections, and exit strategy. Provide a detailed description of the property's potential, renovation plans, and estimated timeline for completion. Clearly state the loan amount, desired terms, and how the funds will be used for the real estate investment. Demonstrate the potential profitability of the project and the borrower's ability to repay the loan.

Once a private lender expresses interest, you will begin with your negotiation and agreement on loan terms.

Interest rate and repayment structure is what both parties are going to be most interested in. I typically use purpose built funds for my private money deals and the funds are structured to provide fund investors with a projected minimum return on their investment. This is the interest that I am paying for these loans but many private money loans with have a more traditional structure and interest rates. Discuss and negotiate the interest rate, repayment schedule, and any other terms relevant to the loan. Factors such as the property's value, borrower's experience, and market conditions can influence these negotiations.

Engage an attorney to review the loan agreement, security

instruments, and other related documents to ensure they align with legal requirements and protect the interests of both parties. The attorney can help identify any potential risks or concerns that need to be addressed before finalizing the loan.

Upon reaching an agreement, the loan closing and disbursement process will take place. Complete all necessary documentation, including promissory notes, security instruments, and loan agreements. Ensure all required signatures and notarization are obtained. Once all closing requirements are met, the agreed-upon funds will be disbursed to the borrower. The funds can be used for the intended purposes, such as property acquisition, renovation, or other investment-related expenses.

Private money loans offer real estate investors a flexible, accessible, and efficient financing option for their investment projects. By understanding the characteristics, advantages, considerations, loan structuring, due diligence, and the application process of private money loans, borrowers can tap into this valuable funding source to achieve their real estate investment goals. Engaging in thorough research, building strong relationships, and working with experienced professionals are key steps to successfully secure private money for real estate investments.

CHAPTER NINE

Owner Financing

Owner financing, also known as seller financing or a purchase money mortgage, is a financing arrangement in real estate where the property seller acts as the lender and provides financing to the buyer. This is also one of my favorite forms of acquiring properties if I can structure the entire transaction favorably. This chapter covers the key aspects of owner financing for real estate investments, including its definition, advantages, considerations, and how to structure and secure owner financing.

Understanding Owner Financing

Owner financing refers to a financing arrangement in which the property seller assumes the role of the lender and extends credit to the buyer for the purchase of the property. The seller receives payments from the buyer, typically in the form of monthly installments, which include principal and interest.

Owner financing possesses unique characteristics that distinguish it from traditional financing options. Owner financing bypasses the need for a traditional lender, allowing the buyer and seller to negotiate and establish the financing terms directly.

Owner financing offers flexibility in terms of interest rates, repayment schedules, and down payment requirements. The terms are negotiable and can be tailored to the specific needs of both parties.

As with many loan strategies, this is an asset-based loan. The property being sold serves as collateral, similar to a traditional mortgage. In case of default, the seller can potentially reclaim the subject property through foreclosure.

Advantages of Owner Financing

Owner financing provides an alternative financing option for buyers who may face challenges obtaining a loan from a traditional lender due to credit history, income limitations, or other factors. It enables buyers to secure financing without relying solely on their creditworthiness.

Owner financing offers flexibility in structuring loan terms. Buyers and sellers have the opportunity to negotiate interest rates, repayment schedules, down payment amounts, and other terms to align with their specific financial situations and investment goals.

Owner financing can expedite the transaction process since it eliminates the need for a traditional lender's approval process, extensive paperwork, and potential delays. The buyer and seller can streamline the process and reach an agreement more quickly.

For sellers, offering owner financing can attract a larger pool of potential buyers who may not qualify for traditional financing. This widens the market and increases the chances of a successful sale. Additionally, sellers can earn interest on the financed amount, potentially increasing their overall return on their investment.

Buyers should carefully assess the following factors before entering into an owner financing arrangement. Buyers should evaluate their financial situation to ensure that they can afford the monthly payments, including principal, interest, and other costs associated with property ownership.

Conduct thorough research on the property, including its condition, market value, and any legal or financial encumbrances. Engage professionals, such as home inspectors and real estate attorneys, to assess the property's condition and legal status.

Work with an attorney to draft a comprehensive purchase agreement and promissory note that clearly outline the terms and conditions of the owner financing arrangement. This helps protect the buyer's rights and ensure compliance with legal requirements.

Sellers should carefully evaluate the following aspects before offering owner financing. Assess the buyer's financial stability, creditworthiness, and ability to make timely payments. Request documentation such as credit reports, income verification, and references to gauge the buyer's reliability.

Implement risk-mitigation strategies, such as conducting thorough due diligence on the buyer, ensuring proper documentation, and securing the property with appropriate legal instruments. Consider requiring a significant down payment to provide a financial cushion in case of default. c. Professional Guidance: Consult with real estate attorneys and professionals experienced in owner financing to ensure compliance with local laws, regulations, and tax implications.

Structuring and Securing Owner Financing

Buyers and sellers should engage in open and transparent negotiations to establish mutually beneficial loan terms. Determine a fair and competitive interest rate based on market conditions, the property's value, and the buyer's creditworthiness. Agree on a repayment schedule that suits both parties, considering the buyer's financial capacity and the seller's desired cash flow. Determine an appropriate down payment amount, which can vary depending on the property's value and the buyer's financial situation.

To protect the interests of both parties, it is essential to draft and execute proper legal documentation. Prepare a comprehensive purchase agreement that outlines the terms and conditions of the sale, including the financing arrangement, property description, purchase price, and any contingencies. Draft a promissory note that specifies the loan amount, interest rate, repayment terms, default provisions, and any other relevant clauses. This serves as evidence of the debt owed by the buyer to the seller.

The closing process for an owner-financed transaction follows a similar procedure to a traditional real estate transaction. Conduct a title search to ensure there are no liens or other encumbrances on the property. Obtain title insurance to protect against any unforeseen issues. Consider using an escrow company to facilitate the transaction and ensure a smooth transfer of funds and legal documents. Record the necessary documents, such as the promissory note and any applicable deeds or mortgages, with the appropriate government authorities to protect the interests of both parties.

Owner financing presents a viable alternative for both buyers and sellers in real estate transactions. Buyers can access financing options that may not be available through traditional lenders, while sellers can expand their potential buyer pool and earn interest on the financed amount. However, it is essential for both parties to conduct due diligence, seek professional guidance, and establish clear terms through comprehensive legal documentation. By understanding the advantages, considerations, and steps involved in owner financing, investors can utilize this financing option to achieve their real estate investment objectives.

CHAPTER TEN

Using an LLC

This chapter is named using an LLC but the same principles apply to an LLP, series LLC and other similar business structures. Understanding the structure an LLC is crucial for a real estate investor. Using LLC's we can secure financing and hold control of our real estate assets.

A Limited Liability Company (LLC) is a type of business entity that combines the advantages of a corporation and a partnership or sole proprietorship. It provides owners, known as members, with limited liability protection while offering flexibility in management and taxation.

An LLC is formed by filing the necessary documents with the appropriate state authority, usually the Secretary of State or similar agency. Once formed, an LLC becomes a separate legal entity, distinct from its owners. This separation allows members to enjoy limited liability, meaning their personal assets are generally protected from the company's debts and liabilities.

One of the key features of an LLC is its flexible management structure. Members have the freedom to choose how the company will be managed. An LLC can be member-managed, where all members actively participate in the decision-making and day-to-day operations, or it can be manager-managed, where one or more designated managers handle the company's affairs while non-managing members have a more passive role.

LLCs are known for their tax flexibility. By default, an LLC is classified as a pass-through entity for tax purposes. This means that the company itself does not pay taxes, but instead, the profits and losses "pass through" to the members, who report them on their individual tax returns. However, LLCs also have the option to choose corporate tax treatment if it better aligns with their financial goals and circumstances.

In terms of governance, LLCs typically have an operating agreement. This document outlines the rights, responsibilities, and operating procedures of the members. It covers various aspects such as profit sharing, voting rights, management structure, decision-making processes, admission of new members, and procedures for dissolution or the departure of a member.

LLCs are a popular choice for small to medium-sized businesses due to their simplicity and flexibility. They are commonly utilized by entrepreneurs, startups, family businesses, professional service providers, and real estate ventures. The absence of complex corporate formalities, such as annual meetings or strict record-keeping requirements, makes LLCs relatively easy to maintain compared to other business structures.

Overall, an LLC provides a favorable blend of liability protection, management flexibility, and tax advantages. It allows business owners to structure their enterprise in a way that suits their specific needs and goals, while also providing a level of personal asset protection.

Funding Through an LLC

Whether you are trying to build funds for leveraging an acquisition or acquiring it outright, LLC's are perfectly suited for funding real estate investments. Members of the LLC can contribute equal or even variable amounts of investment. The investment percentage of each member is typically that of the percentage of investment they have contributed but there is no hard fast rule that states that. The terms and percentages of membership and control, even returns and benefits should all be outlined in the LLC member agreement or contract.

When you have multiple different members in an LLC, you can get hamstrung by multiple different opinions and ideas and these situations can lead to a messy situation. To avoid or at least mitigate such situations, your LLC should have a managing partner, ideally it should be you.

Managing Partner

A managing partner in a Limited Liability Company (LLC) is an individual who holds a position of significant responsibility and authority within the organization. As a managing partner, they play a crucial role in overseeing and directing the operations and strategic direction of the company. Their primary objective is to ensure the success, growth, and profitability of the business.

The managing partner is typically one of the owners or members of the LLC, although it is possible for an outsider to assume this role if agreed upon by the members. They are chosen based on their leadership qualities, expertise, experience, and ability to make sound business decisions. The managing partner's duties and responsibilities can vary depending on the specific needs and structure of the LLC, but generally include the following.

The managing partner takes part in developing the LLC's long-term goals and devises strategies to achieve them. They analyze market trends, assess competition, and make informed decisions to position the LLC for growth and success.

The managing partner ensures that day-to-day operations run smoothly and efficiently. They oversee various aspects of the business, such as production, finance, sales, marketing, and human resources, and may delegate responsibilities to other team members or managers.

The managing partner plays a critical role in financial management, including budgeting, financial forecasting, and monitoring the LLC's financial performance. They make informed decisions regarding investments, cost control measures, and capital allocation.

The managing partner is responsible for making key decisions for the LLC. They evaluate risks, assess potential opportunities, and determine the best course of action. They may consult with other members or stakeholders, but ultimately, the managing partner carries the responsibility of making final decisions.

The managing partner provides leadership and guidance to the LLC's employees, contractors, vendors and suppliers and promotes a positive and collaborative work culture and ensures alignment with the LLC's vision and values. They may recruit and hire new employees, establish performance goals, and provide ongoing feedback and support.

The managing partner ensures that the LLC operates within the legal framework and complies with relevant regulations and requirements. They may work closely with legal counsel to address any legal issues, draft contracts, and protect the company's interests.

The managing partner represents the LLC in external relationships, such as with clients, suppliers, partners, and investors. They maintain strong professional networks, negotiate contracts and agreements, and cultivate positive relationships that contribute to the company's growth and reputation.

Overall, the managing partner in an LLC holds a position of authority and responsibility, steering the company towards its goals and ensuring its overall success. They possess a combination of strategic thinking, leadership skills, business acumen, and a deep understanding of the industry in which the company operates.

When acquiring financing through an LLC, the managing partner should consider their stake in the LLC and the transaction. I have set up many LLC's where I was the managing partner and that position alone provided me with a significant investment stake in the property or properties controlled by the LLC.

CHAPTER ELEVEN

Using a Corporation

Financing and acquiring real estate with a corporation can provide numerous advantages and opportunities for investors. I use corporations across all of my real estate investing and business ventures. A corporation can be used with other business structures to lend even greater asset protection to your personal assets as well as your business and investing assets. Corporation can also provide all kinds of different tax benefits. All of this and more are reasons why I love and use corporations.

There are two different types of corporations, the S or Sub- Chapter S Corporation and the C Corporation. There are distinct differences between both of these types of corporations. Make sure you understand the differences, the benefits and limitations of each and choose which type of corporation you believe is going to be most beneficial to your and your goals.

This chapter explores the key aspects of using a corporation to finance and acquire real estate, including the benefits, considerations, and steps involved in the process. We will cover the advantages of using a corporate structure, financing options available to corporations, due diligence considerations, and the acquisition process.

Benefits of Using a Corporation for Real Estate Investments

One of the primary benefits of using a corporation for real estate investments is the liability protection it provides. A corporation is a separate legal entity, distinct from its owners (shareholders) and is by law considered a person. This separation shields shareholders from personal liability for the debts and obligations of the corporation. In the event of a lawsuit or financial loss, the personal assets of shareholders are protected.

Operating through a corporation can enhance credibility and professionalism in real estate transactions. Potential business partners, lenders, and investors often view corporations as more stable and secure entities, which can lead to favorable financing terms and increased opportunities for growth and expansion.

Corporations benefit from various tax advantages, such as deductions for business expenses, depreciation of real estate assets, and the ability to structure transactions to minimize tax liabilities. Additionally, corporations can offer tax-efficient strategies for estate planning and wealth transfer.

A corporation provides a structure that facilitates capital raising and growth. By issuing shares of stock, a corporation can attract investors and raise funds to finance real estate acquisitions or development projects. The ability to issue equity allows for potential expansion and diversification of real estate holdings.

Financing Options for Corporations

Corporations can seek financing through traditional bank loans. Banks typically evaluate the corporation's financial strength, creditworthiness, and the property's value and potential income. The corporation's financial statements, business plan, and collateral may be required for loan approval.

Commercial mortgages are specifically designed for financing commercial properties owned by corporations. These loans are secured by the property and can provide long-term financing with fixed or variable interest rates. The terms and conditions of commercial mortgages vary, and borrowers may need to meet specific eligibility criteria.

Corporations seeking substantial financing for real estate

investments can explore private equity and venture capital options. These sources of funding involve investors providing capital in exchange for equity or a share of the corporation's profits. Private equity and venture capital firms often specialize in real estate investments and can offer strategic guidance and industry expertise.

Corporations seeking to fund their corporation and or assets can sell shares in the corporation to investors who will then become shareholders in the corporation. This can be done whether the corporation is privately held or is publicly held.

Emerging financing methods, such as real estate crowdfunding and peer-to-peer lending platforms, provide opportunities for corporations to access capital from a broader pool of investors. These platforms connect real estate investors with individuals or groups willing to provide funding for specific projects. This alternative financing approach can offer flexibility and diversification in funding sources.

Make sure you understand the various different corporate structures and compliance requirements. Before financing and acquiring real estate with a corporation, it is crucial to establish and maintain a proper corporate structure. This includes forming the corporation, adhering to all legal and regulatory requirements, and maintaining accurate financial records. Compliance with corporate governance and reporting obligations is essential for preserving the limited liability protection.

The Acquisition Process

Identify suitable real estate opportunities that align with the corporation's investment strategy and goals. Conduct market research, network with industry professionals, and engage real estate agents to identify potential properties. Negotiate purchase terms, price, and conditions to secure the most favorable deal.

Once a property is identified, prepare a comprehensive financing application with the necessary documentation, including financial statements, business plans, property appraisals, and legal documents. Submit the application to the chosen lender or funding source and work closely with them throughout the approval process.

During the closing process, engage a real estate attorney to review and finalize the legal documentation, such as purchase agreements, loan agreements, and property deeds. Ensure compliance with all legal requirements, obtain necessary approvals, and transfer ownership of the property to the corporation. Complete all necessary recording and registration processes with the relevant authorities.

Using a corporation for real estate financing and acquisition offers numerous advantages, including limiting liability, protection, enhanced credibility, and tax benefits. Corporations have access to a wide range of financing options, including traditional bank loans, commercial mortgages, private equity, sales of stock and shares, crowdfunding platforms and more. Careful due diligence, proper corporate structuring, and thorough property analysis are essential to ensure successful real estate investments for your corporation. By understanding the benefits, considerations, and steps involved in financing and acquiring real estate with a corporation, investors can leverage this structure to achieve their investment objectives and build a strong real estate portfolio.

CHAPTER TWELVE

Purpose Built Funds

Throughout these past chapters I've been telling you about different funding strategies that are among my favorite strategies. Now we have arrived at what is currently my number one favorite strategy for funding. An investment fund, funded by investors, built specifically for me and my real estate investing pursuits.

Establishing a fund for real estate investment provides a structured and organized approach for pooling capital from multiple investors to finance and acquire real estate assets. This chapter covers the detailed aspects of setting up a real estate investment fund, including the benefits, considerations, fund structure, regulatory compliance, investor relations, fund management, risk management, and operational processes.

Understanding Real Estate Investment Funds

Real estate investment funds are investment vehicles that allow investors to collectively pool their capital for investing in real estate projects or properties. Each of the funds that I use were established and are managed by a licensed fund manager. My fund managers are also responsible for attracting the investors to provide the funding for each of these funds. They do that with a prospectus that we create together that outlines the types of investments the fund will be investing in, past performances of other funds that we've had and projected returns for a specific fund.

There are different types of real estate investment funds.

Closed-End Funds: These funds have a fixed number of shares or units and operate for a specific period, with limited liquidity for investors.

Open-End Funds: Also known as mutual funds, these funds allow investors to buy or sell shares at any time, offering more liquidity.

Real Estate Investment Trusts (REITs): REITs are publicly traded companies that own and operate income-generating real estate assets. They provide a convenient way for investors to access real estate investments through shares traded on stock exchanges. d. Private Equity Real Estate Funds: These funds typically target higher-net-worth individuals and institutional investors and focus on investing in properties with value-added or opportunistic strategies.

A real estate investment fund enables diversification across multiple properties, locations, and asset classes, reducing investment risk to the investors in the fund.

Investors benefit from the expertise of professional fund managers who conduct thorough market research, property analysis, and asset management. Real estate investment funds provide access to large-scale and high-quality real estate projects that may not be accessible to individual investors. Pooling capital allows the fund to pursue larger acquisitions, negotiate better deals, and access favorable financing terms. Diversification, professional management, and strategic decision-making help mitigate investment risks.

Determine the most suitable structure for the fund, such as a limited partnership, limited liability company (LLC), or another entity type, based on factors like taxation, liability protection, and flexibility. b. Legal Compliance: Consult legal professionals to ensure compliance with local laws, regulations, and securities requirements regarding fund formation, operation, and investor solicitation.

Establish the investment strategy, including property types, geographic focus, risk-return profile, and investment time horizons. Set clear investment objectives, such as income generation, capital appreciation, or a combination of both, aligned with investor expectations.

Fundraising and Investor Relations

Develop a comprehensive fundraising plan, including target investor demographics, marketing materials, a private placement memorandum (PPM), and investor presentations. Establish strong investor relations by providing regular updates, transparent reporting, and clear communication channels to maintain investor confidence.

Implement a robust risk management framework to identify, assess, and mitigate potential risks associated with real estate investments. Ensure compliance with regulatory requirements, including anti-money laundering (AML) and know-your-customer (KYC) protocols, to maintain the fund's reputation and integrity.

Fund Management and Operations

Establish a systematic process for deal sourcing, leveraging industry networks, real estate brokers, and proprietary research to identify potential investment opportunities. Conduct comprehensive due diligence on potential investments, including financial analysis, property inspections, legal reviews, market analysis, and risk assessments.

Implement effective asset management strategies to maximize property performance, optimize rental income, and enhance overall investment returns. Identify value-add opportunities through property renovations, operational improvements, and lease optimization to increase property value.

Establish a robust performance monitoring system to track the fund's financial performance, key performance indicators (KPIs), and investment returns. Provide regular and transparent investor reports, including financial statements, performance updates, property valuations, and fund outlooks.

Develop clear exit strategies for each investment, considering factors such as market conditions, investment objectives, and investor preferences. Plan for fund liquidation by establishing an exit timeline, conducting asset sales, and distributing profits to investors in accordance with the fund's governing documents.

Establishing a real estate investment fund requires careful planning, adherence to legal and regulatory requirements, effective investor relations, and robust fund management practices. By understanding the benefits, considerations, and operational processes involved, you as real estate investors with the right fund managers and structures can successfully navigate the establishment and operation of a real estate investment fund. With a well-defined investment strategy, thorough due diligence, and diligent risk management, a dedicated or purpose build real estate investment fund can provide investors with opportunities for diversification, professional management, and access to attractive real estate investment opportunities while providing you with significant returns.

CHAPTER THIRTEEN

Syndication and Partnerships

Syndication and partnerships are powerful strategies employed by real estate investors to pool resources, share risks, and capitalize on larger investment opportunities. In this comprehensive chapter, we will delve into the concept of syndication and partnerships in real estate investing, exploring their benefits, various structures, and key considerations for successful implementation.

Syndication involves the pooling of capital from multiple investors to acquire, operate, and manage real estate properties. This collaborative approach allows individual investors to participate in deals that may be beyond their financial capabilities or expertise. Syndication can take different forms.

General Partnership

In a general partnership, all partners actively participate in the investment and share both the profits and liabilities. Each partner contributes capital, skills, or both and collectively makes decisions regarding the acquisition, management, and sale of the property.

Limited Partnership (LP)

A limited partnership structure consists of general partners who manage the investment and limited partners who provide capital but have limited decision-making authority. Limited partners are typically passive investors, enjoying limited liability and a share of the profits proportional to their investment.

Limited Liability Company (LLC)

An LLC is a flexible business structure that combines elements of partnerships and corporations. It offers limited liability protection to its members while allowing for the allocation of profits and losses based on the partnership agreement.

Benefits of Syndication and Partnerships

Syndication and partnerships offer numerous advantages for real estate investors. Some of the key benefits include:

Access to Larger Deals

By pooling resources, investors gain access to larger real estate projects that may provide higher returns on investment. This allows for diversification and the potential to participate in properties with significant growth potential.

Shared Expertise

Syndication and partnerships enable investors to leverage the expertise, skills, and experience of other partners. Each partner brings unique knowledge and resources to the table, increasing the likelihood of making informed investment decisions and optimizing property performance.

Risk Mitigation

Sharing the financial burden and risks among multiple investors helps to mitigate individual risk exposure. This collective approach provides a sense of security, as losses are spread across multiple participants, reducing the impact on any single investor.

Enhanced Deal-Making Power

Syndication and partnerships often attract favorable financing terms and enhance negotiating power. Lenders and sellers may be more willing to collaborate with a group of investors, offering better loan terms, more attractive purchase prices, and access to off-market opportunities.

Increased Deal Flow

Participating in a syndication or partnership network provides access to a wider range of investment opportunities and deal flow. Collaborating with other investors allows for the sharing of leads, connections, and industry knowledge, increasing the chances of identifying attractive investments.

Key Considerations for Syndication and Partnerships

Clear Investment Strategy: Defining a clear investment strategy is crucial to guide the syndication or partnership. Outline the property type, location preferences, target returns, risk tolerance, and expected holding period. This establishes a framework that aligns the objectives and expectations of all partners.

Trust and Compatibility

Building trust and establishing compatibility among partners is essential for the success of a syndication or partnership. Conduct thorough due diligence on potential partners, assess their track record, communication style, and values to ensure alignment in goals, vision, and risk appetite.

Legal Structure and Documentation

Seek legal advice to determine the most appropriate legal structure for your syndication or partnership. Draft comprehensive partnership agreements or operating agreements that clearly define the roles, responsibilities, profit-sharing mechanisms, decision-making processes, and exit strategies.

Communication and Decision-Making

Establish clear communication channels and decision-making protocols within the syndication or partnership. Regular and transparent communication among partners is essential for effective collaboration, conflict resolution, and problem-solving.

Investor Relations

Developing a robust investor relations strategy is crucial when working with limited partners. Timely and transparent communication regarding investment performance, financials, and major decisions helps maintain trust and fosters long-term partnerships.

Exit Strategy

Define the exit strategy upfront, including the anticipated holding period and options for exiting the investment. This ensures that all partners are aligned on the long-term objectives and expectations, reducing potential conflicts during the exit process.

Syndication Management and Compliance

Effectively managing a syndication or partnership requires careful oversight and compliance with legal and regulatory requirements. Consider the following aspects:

Securities Laws

Syndication structures may fall under securities regulations. Seek guidance from legal professionals well-versed in securities laws to ensure compliance with applicable regulations, such as the Securities Act of 1933 and the Securities Exchange Act of 1934.

Reporting and Compliance

Maintain accurate records, financial statements, and investor communications in compliance with legal and regulatory requirements. Appoint qualified professionals, such as certified public accountants and attorneys, to handle financial reporting, tax obligations, and ongoing compliance needs.

Investor Due Diligence

Conduct thorough due diligence on potential investors to comply with anti-money laundering (AML) and know-your-customer (KYC) regulations. Implement appropriate processes to verify the identity and suitability of investors in alignment with legal requirements.

Ongoing Compliance

Stay informed about changes in securities laws and regulations to ensure ongoing compliance. Regularly review and update internal processes, procedures, and documentation to adhere to legal requirements and best practices.

Syndication and partnerships offer real estate investors an avenue to leverage resources, expertise, and opportunities beyond their individual capabilities. By participating in syndication or forming strategic partnerships, investors can access larger deals, share risks, and potentially achieve higher returns. However, successful syndication and partnerships require careful planning, clear communication, and compliance with legal and regulatory obligations. By considering the benefits and key considerations outlined in this chapter, you will be well-equipped to make informed decisions and navigate the intricacies of syndication and partnerships in real estate investing.

Finding the right partners is a critical aspect of real estate investing syndication. The success of your syndication venture depends on the collective expertise, resources, and shared vision of the partners involved. In this extensive and detailed chapter, we will explore a comprehensive approach to identifying potential partners for real estate investing syndication. We will delve into the key considerations, strategies, and resources that will help you identify partners who align with your investment goals and contribute to the overall success of your syndication.

Define Your Investment Criteria

Before embarking on the search for partners, it is important to define your investment criteria. Consider the following factors:

Investment Strategy

Clarify your investment strategy, such as property types (residential, commercial, industrial), location preferences, risk tolerance, and targeted returns. This will help you identify partners who have a similar investment focus.

Expertise and Skills

Determine the specific expertise and skills you bring to the table, such as property acquisition, financial analysis, asset management, or marketing. Identify areas where you may need additional expertise and seek partners who can complement your skill set.

Financial Capacity

Assess your own financial capacity and the amount of capital you can contribute to the syndication. This will help you evaluate potential partners' financial resources and ensure they can bring sufficient capital to the table.

Network within the Real Estate Community

Networking is a powerful tool for identifying potential partners. Expand your network within the real estate community by employing the following strategies:

Attend Industry Events

Attend real estate conferences, seminars, workshops, and local meetups. These events provide opportunities to connect with like-minded professionals, including potential partners. Engage in conversations, exchange business cards, and build relationships.

Join Real Estate Associations and Groups

Become a member of real estate associations, investment clubs, or online communities. Participate actively, contribute valuable insights, and connect with other members who share your investment goals.

Seek Referrals

Reach out to trusted contacts within the industry, such as real estate agents, brokers, attorneys, or lenders. Let them know you are looking for potential partners for real estate syndication. They may be able to refer you to individuals who are interested in syndication opportunities.

Utilize Online Platforms

Leverage online platforms and social media networks dedicated to real estate investing. Join relevant groups, participate in discussions, and connect with potential partners who are active in these online communities.

Conduct Extensive Research

Thorough research is crucial to identify potential partners who align with your investment goals and have a strong track record. Consider the following steps:

Online Research

Utilize online resources, such as professional networking platforms and industry directories, to identify individuals who have experience in real estate investing or syndication. Review their profiles, professional backgrounds, and accomplishments.

Analyze Market Presence

Look for individuals who have a strong market presence, such as those who regularly contribute articles, speak at industry conferences, or host educational webinars. This indicates their knowledge and expertise in real estate investing.

Review Past Syndication Deals

Analyze past syndication deals or partnerships that potential partners have been involved in. Assess the performance of these ventures, including the acquisition process, asset management, and overall returns. This will help you evaluate their track record and expertise.

Attend Local Real Estate Meetings

Participate in local real estate meetings, property auctions, or investment group gatherings. Engage with other investors and syndicators to gain insights into their experiences and potential partnership opportunities.

Evaluate Potential Partners

Once you have identified potential partners, it is important to evaluate them thoroughly.

Track Record and Experience

Evaluate the track record and experience of potential partners in real estate investing, syndication, and relevant roles such as acquisitions, property management, or financing. Look for partners who have a proven history of success and align with your investment strategy.

Financial Capability

Assess the financial capacity of potential partners to ensure they can contribute the necessary capital to the syndication. Request financial statements or proof of funds to verify their ability to meet financial commitments.

Compatibility and Shared Vision

Assess the compatibility and shared vision between you and potential partners. Evaluate their communication style, work ethic, and commitment to the syndication venture. Look for partners who share similar values and goals.

References and Background Checks

Seek references from individuals who have worked with potential partners in the past. Contact previous business associates, colleagues, or partners to gain insights into their reputation, professionalism, and integrity. Conduct thorough background checks, including criminal and credit history, to ensure you are partnering with trustworthy individuals.

Leverage Professional Resources

Engaging professional resources can provide valuable guidance and support in identifying potential partners. Consider the following:

Real Estate Attorneys

Seek advice from real estate attorneys who specialize in syndication and partnership agreements. They can help review legal documents, draft partnership agreements, and ensure compliance with applicable laws.

Accountants and Financial Advisors

Consult with accountants and financial advisors to evaluate the financial aspects of potential partners. They can assist in analyzing their financial stability, tax implications, and overall financial health.

Industry Consultants

Engage industry consultants who specialize in real estate investing or syndication. They can provide valuable insights, market trends, and guidance on identifying potential partners based on their extensive experience in the field.

Identifying potential partners for real estate investing syndication requires a comprehensive and strategic approach. By defining your investment criteria, expanding your network within the real estate community, conducting extensive research, evaluating potential partners, and leveraging professional resources, you can find partners who align with your investment goals and contribute to the success of your syndication venture. Remember, selecting the right partners is crucial for building a strong foundation and maximizing the potential of your real estate investments.

A well-crafted syndication or partnership agreement is essential for establishing a clear and mutually beneficial framework for real estate investing ventures. This chapter provides an in-depth exploration of the key components, considerations, and best practices involved in developing a comprehensive syndication or partnership agreement. By understanding the intricacies of this agreement, you can protect your interests, establish clear guidelines, and foster a successful collaboration with your partners.

The Importance of a Syndication or Partnership Agreement

A syndication or partnership agreement serves as a legally binding document that outlines the terms, conditions, and responsibilities of all parties involved in a real estate investment venture. It provides a framework for decision-making, profit sharing, dispute resolution, and exit strategies. The agreement helps establish clear expectations, mitigates risks, and enhances the overall effectiveness of the syndication or partnership.

Key Components of a Syndication or Partnership Agreement: Developing a comprehensive syndication or partnership agreement involves including several key components. Consider the following elements:

Introduction and Background

Provide an introduction to the agreement, outlining the purpose, objectives, and background of the syndication or partnership. This section should also define the legal entities involved and their roles.

Definitions and Interpretation

Define key terms and concepts used throughout the agreement to ensure clarity and avoid misunderstandings. Provide clear interpretations of the terms to avoid ambiguity.

Roles and Responsibilities

Clearly outline the roles and responsibilities of each party involved in the syndication or partnership. Specify the tasks and obligations related to property acquisition, financing, asset management, reporting, and decision-making.

Capital Contributions

Detail the capital contributions required from each partner, including the amount, timing, and method of payment. Establish guidelines for additional capital calls, if necessary, and address how profits and losses will be allocated among partners.

Profit Sharing and Distribution

Define the profit-sharing structure, including the distribution of profits, returns on investment, and any preferred returns or hurdles. Specify the frequency and method of profit distribution.

Decision-Making Process

Establish a decision-making process that outlines how major decisions will be made within the syndication or partnership. Define voting rights, thresholds, and procedures for resolving disagreements or deadlock situations.

Management and Operations

Determine the management structure and responsibilities for the syndication or partnership. Specify the decision-making authority, property management, leasing, maintenance, and reporting requirements.

Exit Strategies and Dissolution

Address exit strategies and contingencies, including the sale of assets, refinancing, or dissolution of the syndication or partnership. Define the process, timing, and distribution of proceeds in the event of an exit or dissolution.

Dispute Resolution

Include provisions for dispute resolution, such as mediation or arbitration, to resolve any conflicts or disagreements between partners. Define the process and the governing law under which disputes will be resolved.

Confidentiality and Non-Compete

Establish confidentiality obligations to protect sensitive information shared within the syndication or partnership. Include non-compete clauses to prevent partners from engaging in similar ventures during the term of the agreement.

Governing Law and Jurisdiction

Specify the governing law and jurisdiction that will govern the agreement. This ensures consistency and provides a legal framework for resolving any disputes.

Considerations in Developing the Agreement

When developing a syndication or partnership agreement, consider the following factors to ensure its effectiveness:

Legal Counsel

Seek the guidance of an experienced real estate attorney specializing in syndication and partnership agreements. They can provide valuable insights, ensure legal compliance, and draft a robust agreement that protects your interests.

Alignment of Interests

Ensure that the agreement aligns the interests of all parties involved. This includes addressing any potential conflicts of interest, defining shared goals, and establishing mechanisms for resolving disputes.

Flexibility and Adaptability

Create an agreement that allows for flexibility and adaptation as circumstances change. Include provisions for amendments, exit strategies, or the addition of new partners if necessary.

Communication and Reporting

Define reporting requirements to keep all partners informed about the progress and performance of the syndication or partnership.

Regular communication and transparency are crucial for maintaining trust and fostering effective collaboration.

Compliance and Regulations

Ensure the agreement complies with all relevant laws, regulations, and securities requirements. Seek advice from legal and financial professionals to navigate any regulatory considerations.

Contingency Plans

Develop contingency plans to address unforeseen circumstances, such as changes in market conditions, partnership dissolution, or the departure of key partners. These plans provide a road-map for handling unexpected situations.

Review and Revision

A syndication or partnership agreement is not a static document. It is important to regularly review and revise the agreement as circumstances evolve. Consider conducting periodic reviews with all partners to ensure that the agreement remains relevant, addresses any new challenges, and aligns with the goals and objectives of the syndication or partnership.

Developing a real estate investing syndication or partnership agreement is a crucial step in establishing a successful collaboration. By incorporating key components, considering important factors, and seeking legal guidance, you can create a comprehensive agreement that protects the interests of all parties involved, fosters effective decision-making, and enhances the overall performance of the syndication or partnership. Remember to regularly review and revise the agreement to adapt to changing circumstances and maintain a strong foundation for your real estate investment ventures.

CHAPTER FOURTEEN

Real Estate Crowd Funding

In recent years, real estate crowdfunding has emerged as a popular and accessible method for individuals to invest in the real estate market. Traditionally, investing in real estate required significant capital and expertise. However, with the advent of crowdfunding platforms, real estate investments have become more inclusive and available to a wider range of investors. This chapter is all about understanding real estate crowdfunding, it's benefits, risks, and the factors to consider before participating in such investments.

What is Real Estate Crowdfunding?

Real estate crowdfunding refers to the practice of raising funds from a large number of individuals, typically through an online platform, to finance real estate projects. These projects can include residential or commercial properties, development projects, or even real estate investment trusts (REITs). Crowdfunding platforms act as intermediaries, connecting investors with real estate developers seeking capital for their projects.

Real estate crowdfunding platforms provide a marketplace where investors can browse and select investment opportunities based on their preferences. Investors can contribute funds towards a specific project, and once the project reaches its funding goal, the funds are transferred to the developer. In return, investors receive a proportional ownership stake in the project or a predetermined return on their investment. Some platforms also offer secondary markets where investors can buy and sell their shares in completed projects.

Benefits of Real Estate Crowdfunding

One of the significant benefits of real estate crowdfunding is the access it provides to a broader range of individuals who may not have had access to the real estate market before. Investors can diversify their portfolios by investing in various projects across different locations and property types. This diversification can help mitigate risks and potentially enhance returns.

Crowdfunding platforms often have lower minimum investment requirements compared to traditional real estate investments. This allows individuals to participate in real estate projects with smaller amounts of capital. Investors can pool their resources with others to collectively fund larger projects, enabling them to access opportunities that would have been out of reach individually.

Investing in real estate crowdfunding can provide investors with a passive income stream in the form of rental income or project profits. Many projects generate ongoing cash flow, such as rental properties or income-producing commercial real estate. Additionally, it offers an avenue for diversifying investment portfolios beyond stocks and bonds, potentially reducing risk.

Crowdfunding platforms often provide detailed information about investment opportunities, including property details, financial projections, and risk assessments. This transparency allows investors to make more informed decisions and conduct thorough due diligence before committing funds.

Investors in real estate crowdfunding typically have limited control over the management and decision-making process of the underlying projects. Decisions related to property management, leasing, and project execution are usually made by the developer or the platform itself. Investors should carefully review the project documents and understand their level of influence or control before investing.

Real estate investments are subject to market fluctuations, and the value of the underlying properties can rise or fall. Economic downturns or changes in local real estate markets can impact the profitability of crowdfunding investments. Investors should assess the market conditions, demand-supply dynamics, and the overall economic outlook before investing.

Investors must carefully evaluate the credibility and track record of the crowdfunding platform before committing funds. Platforms may vary in terms of transparency, due diligence, investor protection mechanisms, and the quality of projects listed. Conducting thorough research on the platform's history, past performance, and investor feedback is crucial to mitigate platform-specific risks.

Real estate crowdfunding is subject to securities regulations that vary across jurisdictions. It is essential for investors to understand the legal framework and compliance requirements imposed by the relevant authorities in their country or region. Some countries may have specific restrictions or regulations that govern crowdfunding activities, including investment limits for individual investors or accreditation requirements.

Investors should thoroughly assess the investment opportunities presented on crowdfunding platforms. Factors such as location, market demand, project feasibility, developer experience, financial projections, and exit strategies should be considered before making an investment decision. Analyzing the project's risk-return profile and conducting property-specific research can help investors make informed choices.

Researching the credibility and reputation of the crowdfunding platform is crucial. Investors should review the platform's track record, past project performance, investor feedback, and the platform's compliance with regulatory requirements. Understanding the platform's due diligence process, investor protections, and dispute resolution mechanisms can help mitigate platform-related risks.

Real estate crowdfunding is subject to securities regulations that vary across jurisdictions. Investors should familiarize themselves with the legal requirements, such as registration or licensing obligations for platforms and investor eligibility criteria. Understanding the regulatory landscape can help investors make compliant investment decisions and protect their interests.

Investors should also evaluate the investor protection mechanisms provided by the crowdfunding platform. This may include escrow services for fund handling, clear communication channels, investor education resources, and dispute resolution procedures. Understanding the platform's commitment to investor protection can provide confidence and peace of mind.

Real estate crowdfunding has democratized real estate investing, offering opportunities for individuals to participate in the market with lower capital requirements. However, it is crucial for investors to conduct thorough research, evaluate risks, and select reputable platforms before making investment decisions. By understanding the intricacies of real estate crowdfunding, investors can navigate this emerging investment avenue more effectively and potentially reap the benefits of a diversified real estate portfolio.

Using Crowdfunding for Real Estate Investment

In recent years, crowdfunding has emerged as an innovative and accessible method for financing various ventures, including real estate investments. In this chapter we'll cover how to use crowdfunding and how it can be effectively utilized to finance real estate projects and the key steps involved in launching a successful crowdfunding campaign for real estate investments.

Choosing the appropriate crowdfunding platform is crucial for the success of a real estate crowdfunding campaign. Consider factors such as the platform's reputation, track record, investor base, fees, and the types of real estate projects they offer. Research multiple platforms and compare their features and services to find the one that aligns with your investment goals and preferences.

Project sponsors need to create a compelling investment proposal to attract potential investors. The proposal should include detailed information about the project, such as location, property type, financial projections, investment structure, and potential risks. Clear and transparent communication is vital to building investor confidence. Additionally, incorporating professional-quality visuals, such as architectural renderings or property images, can enhance the presentation of the investment opportunity.

Successful crowdfunding campaigns require effective marketing and investor outreach strategies. Utilize various marketing channels, including social media, email marketing, and targeted advertising, to raise awareness about the investment opportunity. Engage with potential investors through webinars, conferences, and one-on-one meetings to answer questions and address concerns. Building a strong network of potential investors and leveraging existing relationships can also contribute to the success of the crowdfunding campaign.

Maintaining good investor relations is crucial throughout the investment period. Provide regular updates on the project's progress, financial performance, and any significant developments. Transparent reporting and communication foster trust and confidence among investors. Timely responses to investor inquiries and providing a dedicated point of contact can further enhance investor satisfaction.

Types of Crowdfunding for Real Estate

There are two primary types of crowdfunding models used in real estate investments, Equity Based Crowdfunding and Debt Based Crowdfunding.

Equity-based crowdfunding is a popular model used in real estate investments, allowing investors to contribute funds in exchange for ownership equity in a specific project. This section explores the key aspects of equity-based crowdfunding and highlights its benefits and considerations.

In equity-based crowdfunding, real estate projects are typically divided into shares or units, and investors purchase these shares or units in exchange for their investment. As a result, investors become partial owners of the property and have a proportional claim to the property's income and potential appreciation.

Benefits of Equity-Based Crowdfunding

Equity-based crowdfunding allows investors to participate in the potential upside of a real estate project. If the project performs well and experiences capital appreciation, investors can benefit from higher returns compared to debt-based crowdfunding models. Investors can earn profits through rental income distributions and the sale of the property.

Equity-based crowdfunding provides an opportunity to diversify real estate investment portfolios. Investors can allocate funds across multiple projects, thereby spreading their risk. By participating in different types of real estate projects, such as residential, commercial, or industrial properties, investors can mitigate the impact of any single project's performance on their overall portfolio.

Similar to other crowdfunding models, equity-based crowdfunding offers a passive investment opportunity. Investors rely on the expertise of project sponsors and professional property managers to handle the day-to-day operations and property management. This allows investors to benefit from real estate investments without the need for active involvement.

Equity-based crowdfunding carries a higher risk profile compared to debt-based models. As partial owners, investors are exposed to market fluctuations, project-specific risks, and other variables that can affect the property's performance. It is essential for investors to carefully assess the risk factors associated with each investment opportunity and diversify their portfolios accordingly.

Equity-based crowdfunding investments in real estate often have a longer investment horizon compared to other investment options. Real estate projects typically require time for development, construction, and stabilization before investors can realize their returns. Investors should be prepared to have their capital tied up for an extended period and align their investment goals with the project's timeline.

Investments in equity-based crowdfunding are generally illiquid. Unlike publicly traded securities, it can be challenging to sell or exit an investment before the completion of the project. Investors should carefully evaluate their liquidity needs and consider the potential for capital lock-up until the property is sold or an exit opportunity arises.

Key Steps for Launching an Equity-Based Crowdfunding Campaign

Project sponsors should conduct thorough feasibility studies to assess the viability of the real estate project. This includes evaluating market demand, conducting financial analyses, and preparing the necessary project documentation, such as business plans, pro forma financials, and legal agreements.

Choose a reputable crowdfunding platform that specializes in equity-based real estate crowdfunding. Research and compare platforms based on their track record, investor base, fees, and support services. The platform should align with the project's specific needs and target investor audience.

Develop a comprehensive investment proposal that highlights the project's unique selling points, including location, property type, target market, financial projections, and risk factors. The proposal should effectively communicate the value proposition and potential returns to attract potential investors.

Implement a robust marketing strategy to reach potential investors. Utilize various channels, such as social media, online advertising, email marketing, and industry events, to generate interest and drive traffic to the crowdfunding campaign. Engage with potential investors through webinars, meetings, and other communication channels to address their questions and concerns.

Maintain open and transparent communication with investors throughout the investment period. Provide regular updates on the project's progress, financial performance, and any significant developments. Establish effective reporting mechanisms to ensure investors are well-informed and feel engaged in the project.

Equity-based crowdfunding provides individual investors with the opportunity to participate in real estate projects as partial owners. This model offers potential for higher returns, portfolio diversification, and passive investment. However, it is crucial for investors to evaluate the associated risks, understand the long-term investment horizon, and consider liquidity considerations. Project sponsors should focus on conducting feasibility studies, selecting the right crowdfunding platform, crafting compelling investment proposals, and implementing effective marketing and investor relations strategies. By following these steps, investors and project sponsors can leverage equity-based crowdfunding to finance real estate investments successfully.

Debt-based crowdfunding is another prominent model used in real estate investments, allowing investors to lend money to a specific project in exchange for periodic interest payments. This section explores the key aspects of debt-based crowdfunding and highlights its benefits and considerations.

How Debt-Based Crowdfunding Works

In debt-based crowdfunding, investors act as lenders and provide loans to real estate projects. These loans are typically secured by the property itself, offering a level of security for investors. In return for their investment, investors receive regular interest payments throughout the loan term.

Benefits of Debt-Based Crowdfunding

Debt-based crowdfunding offers investors predictable and regular income in the form of interest payments. Investors receive fixed or variable interest payments based on the terms of the loan agreement. This consistent cash flow can be particularly attractive for income-focused investors.

Compared to equity-based crowdfunding, debt-based crowdfunding carries a lower risk profile. As lenders, investors have a higher priority claim on the project's cash flow and assets in case of default. The loan is typically secured by the property, providing investors with a degree of protection. However, it's important to note that all investments carry inherent risks, and investors should conduct proper due diligence.

Debt-based crowdfunding investments often have shorter investment horizons compared to equity-based models. Loans are typically repaid within a defined period, ranging from several months to a few years. This shorter timeline allows investors to potentially recycle their capital more quickly, providing flexibility in deploying funds into other investment opportunities.

Debt-based crowdfunding typically offers lower potential returns compared to equity-based models. As lenders, investors are primarily focused on receiving interest payments and the return of their principal. While the risk profile is lower, the upside potential in terms of capital appreciation is limited compared to equity-based investments.

Investing in debt-based crowdfunding carries the risk of borrower default or delays in repayment. It is essential for investors to evaluate the creditworthiness and financial stability of the borrower or project sponsor. Thorough due diligence, including analyzing the borrower's financials, credit history, and project feasibility, can help mitigate default risk.

Debt-based crowdfunding often involves various loan structures, such as fixed-rate loans, variable-rate loans, or mezzanine financing. It is crucial for investors to educate themselves on the specific loan terms, including interest rates, repayment schedules, and any associated fees. Understanding the loan structure is essential for assessing the investment's potential returns and risks accurately.

Key Steps for Launching a Debt-Based Crowdfunding Campaign

Project sponsors should conduct thorough feasibility studies to assess the viability of the real estate project. This includes evaluating market demand, conducting financial analyses, and preparing the necessary project documentation, such as business plans, financial projections, and legal agreements.

Choose a reputable crowdfunding platform that specializes in debt-based real estate crowdfunding. Research and compare platforms based on their track record, investor base, fees, and support services. The platform should align with the project's specific needs and target investor audience.

Develop a compelling loan offering that outlines the key terms and conditions, including interest rates, repayment schedules, and any associated fees. Clearly communicate the project's financial projections, risk factors, and the collateral securing the loan. Providing transparent and detailed information helps investors make informed lending decisions.

Implement a comprehensive marketing strategy to attract potential investors. Utilize various marketing channels, such as digital advertising, industry events, and targeted outreach, to reach potential lenders. Highlight the investment's attractive features, such as the projected interest rate, security measures, and the project's potential.

Maintain regular and transparent communication with investors throughout the loan term. Provide updates on the project's progress, financial performance, and any significant developments. Establish effective reporting mechanisms to ensure investors are informed about the project's performance and repayment status.

Debt-based crowdfunding provides investors with the opportunity to lend money to real estate projects and receive regular interest payments. This model offers predictable income, a lower risk profile, and shorter investment horizons. However, investors should consider the potential for lower returns, default risk, and educate themselves on loan structures. Project sponsors should focus on conducting feasibility studies, selecting the right crowdfunding platform, crafting comprehensive loan offerings, and implementing effective marketing and investor relations strategies. By following these steps, investors and project sponsors can leverage debt-based crowdfunding to finance real estate investments successfully.

Crowdfunding has emerged as a game-changer in the real estate investment landscape, offering individual investors the opportunity to participate in projects that were previously out of reach. Through crowdfunding, investors can access diverse real estate opportunities, benefit from professional management, and potentially earn attractive returns. However, it is important to understand the regulatory landscape, assess the risks and returns carefully, and select the right crowdfunding platform. By following the key steps outlined in this chapter and conducting thorough due diligence, investors and project sponsors can navigate the world of crowdfunding to finance their real estate investments successfully.

CHAPTER FIFTEEN

Creating A Business Plan

Creating a comprehensive business plan for multi-family property investing is an essential step in the investment process. A well-designed business plan can help investors identify potential risks, evaluate the financial feasibility of the investment, and create a road-map for success. In this chapter, we will provide a more detailed overview of the key components of a business plan for multi-family property investing.

- Executive Summary
- Market Analysis
- Investment Strategy
- Financial Projections
- Marketing Plan
- Management Plan
- Risk Analysis

Executive Summary

A business plan executive summary is a concise and compelling overview of a full business plan. It serves as an introduction to the plan, providing a snapshot of the key elements and capturing the reader's attention. The purpose of an executive summary is to convey the essence of the business plan and entice readers to delve deeper into the document.

Typically, an executive summary includes essential information about the business, such as its mission, product or service offering, target market, competitive advantage, marketing and sales strategies, financial projections, and growth potential. It highlights the most critical aspects of the business plan, emphasizing its unique value proposition and the potential for success.

The executive summary should be concise, usually ranging from one to three pages, and should be written in a clear and compelling manner. It should provide a high-level overview of the business, highlighting the most crucial points without delving into excessive detail. The summary should be engaging and capture the reader's attention from the start, motivating them to continue reading the full business plan.

While the executive summary is placed at the beginning of the business plan, it is often the last section to be written. This allows the writer to summarize and distill the key information and highlights from the complete plan, ensuring that the summary is aligned with the detailed content that follows.

Overall, a business plan executive summary is a powerful tool that encapsulates the essence of the business plan, showcasing the viability, potential, and attractiveness of the venture. It serves as a crucial document for investors, lenders, partners, and other stakeholders who need a quick overview of the business and its prospects.

Market Analysis

A business plan market plan is a section within a comprehensive business plan that outlines the company's marketing strategies and approaches to reach and engage its target market. It provides a road-map for the business to effectively promote its products or services, attract customers, and achieve its revenue and growth objectives.

The market plan begins with a thorough analysis of the target market, including demographics, psychographics, and market trends. This analysis helps the business understand its customers' needs, preferences, and behaviors, enabling the development of targeted marketing initiatives.

Within the market plan, the business identifies its unique value proposition and competitive advantage. It highlights the features, benefits, and differentiation of its products or services compared to competitors, positioning the business effectively in the market.

The market plan outlines the marketing strategies and tactics that the business will employ to create brand awareness, generate leads, and drive sales. It includes the channels through which the business will reach its target audience, such as digital marketing, traditional advertising, social media, public relations, direct marketing, or partnerships.

The plan also details the pricing strategy, including pricing models, discounts, and incentives, considering the competitive landscape and the perceived value of the offerings.

Furthermore, the market plan addresses customer relationship management, outlining how the business will nurture and maintain relationships with its customers. It may include strategies for customer retention, loyalty programs, customer support, and gathering customer feedback.

Metrics and analytics play a crucial role in the market plan as well. The plan identifies the key performance indicators (KPIs) that will be tracked to measure the effectiveness of the marketing efforts. This may include metrics such as customer acquisition cost (CAC), conversion rates, customer lifetime value (CLV), and return on marketing investment (ROMI).

In summary, a business plan market plan is a strategic document that outlines the company's marketing objectives, strategies, and tactics. It provides a road-map for the business to effectively navigate the market, attract and retain customers, and achieve its revenue goals. The market plan is essential for aligning the marketing activities with the overall business strategy and ensuring a focused and cohesive approach to market the products or services effectively.

Investment Strategy

A business plan investment strategy outlines the approach a company intends to take to secure funding or investments to support its operations, growth, and strategic initiatives. It serves as a road-map for attracting investors by clearly presenting the business's financial needs, potential returns, and the benefits of investing in the company.

The investment strategy section of a business plan typically includes several key elements. Firstly, it provides a comprehensive overview of the funding requirements, specifying the amount of capital needed, the purpose of the investment, and the timeline for the funding. This section also outlines the allocation of funds, detailing how the investment will be used to support various aspects of the business, such as research and development, marketing, operational expenses, or expansion plans.

Furthermore, the investment strategy highlights the potential returns and benefits for investors. It presents a compelling case by showcasing the company's growth prospects, market opportunities, and competitive advantage. This may include financial projections, revenue forecasts, and a detailed analysis of the market and industry trends, demonstrating the potential for profitability and long-term success.

In addition, the investment strategy addresses the company's valuation and the proposed terms for the investment. It provides information on the ownership structure, equity or debt financing options, and the potential exit strategies for investors, such as an initial public offering (IPO), acquisition, or buyback.

Moreover, the business plan investment strategy should clearly articulate the value proposition for potential investors. It highlights the unique aspects of the business, such as proprietary technology, intellectual property, market traction, or a strong management team, that make it an attractive investment opportunity. This section may also include testimonials, case studies, or market validation to build credibility and confidence among investors.

Lastly, the investment strategy addresses the marketing and outreach efforts to attract potential investors. It outlines the targeted investor profile, whether it's angel investors, venture capitalists, private equity firms, or strategic partners, and describes the channels and networks the company will leverage to reach and engage with these investors. This may include attending industry conferences, leveraging personal networks, engaging with investment platforms, or working with investment bankers or advisors.

In summary, a business plan investment strategy is a critical section that outlines the company's funding requirements, potential returns, and the benefits of investing in the business. It presents a compelling case for investors, showcasing the growth prospects, market opportunities, and competitive advantage of the company. By addressing the financial needs, valuation, and outreach efforts, the investment strategy aims to secure the necessary funding to support the company's operations and fuel its growth trajectory.

Financial Projections

A business plan financial projection is a critical component of a comprehensive business plan that provides a forecast of the company's financial performance over a specific period. It offers a glimpse into the expected revenue, expenses, and profitability of the business, helping stakeholders assess its financial viability and potential return on investment.

Financial projections typically cover a specific timeframe, such as one to five years, and include various financial statements and key financial metrics. The primary financial statements included in the projections are the income statement, balance sheet, and cash flow statement.

The income statement, also known as the profit and loss statement, outlines the projected revenues, cost of goods sold, operating expenses, and net income or loss. It provides an overview of the company's expected sales volumes, pricing strategy, direct costs, and overhead expenses, allowing stakeholders to assess the business's profitability and revenue growth trajectory.

The balance sheet presents the company's projected assets, liabilities, and shareholders' equity at a given point in time. It includes information on the company's expected cash, accounts receivable, inventory, accounts payable, long-term debt, and equity.

The balance sheet provides insights into the business's financial position, liquidity, and solvency, helping stakeholders assess its ability to meet its financial obligations and sustain its operations.

The cash flow statement projects the company's anticipated cash inflows and outflows during the specified period. It highlights the cash generated from operating activities, investing activities, and financing activities. The cash flow statement is crucial for understanding the company's cash position, its ability to fund operations and investments, and its cash flow dynamics.

In addition to the financial statements, financial projections often include key financial metrics and ratios that help evaluate the company's financial health and performance. These may include metrics such as gross margin, net profit margin, return on investment (ROI), return on equity (ROE), and break-even analysis.

Financial projections are typically based on various assumptions, such as market demand, pricing, cost structures, and industry trends. These assumptions should be supported by thorough market research and analysis to ensure their reasonability and accuracy.

Financial projections serve multiple purposes, including attracting investors, securing financing, guiding internal financial planning, and monitoring the business's financial performance against the projected targets. They provide stakeholders with a clear understanding of the expected financial outcomes and help make informed decisions about the business's future.

Developing a budget and financial projections is a crucial step in creating a business plan for multi-family investing. It helps investors determine the feasibility of their investment goals and develop a realistic plan for achieving them. Here are some more detailed steps you can take to establish a budget and financial projections for your multi-family investing venture:

Before you start investing, it's essential to determine how much money you have available to invest. This could include your own funds, as well as any loans or financing options you may be considering. It's important to be realistic about your budget and to take into account all the costs associated with the investment, including property acquisition, renovations, and ongoing maintenance.

Once you've determined your budget, you can start estimating your revenue. This will be based on the rental income you expect to generate from the properties. Research the market and analyze comparable rental properties to determine a fair rental rate for your units. You may also want to consider other sources of income, such as laundry facilities or parking.

In addition to property acquisition and renovation costs, you'll need to calculate your ongoing expenses, such as property taxes, insurance, utilities, and maintenance. Be sure to account for all of these expenses in your budget to ensure that you have a realistic projection of your cash flow. It's also important to consider any unexpected expenses that may arise, such as repairs or legal fees.

With your revenue and expenses estimated, you can create financial projections for your multi-family investing venture. This will include cash flow projections, income statements, and balance sheets. Be sure to account for any fluctuations in income or expenses, such as vacancies or unexpected repairs. You may want to consider using a spreadsheet or financial software to create and manage your projections.

Once you have your financial projections in place, you can assess your expected return on investment (ROI). This will give you a clear idea of the profitability of your investment and help you determine whether the investment is worth pursuing. You may also want to consider other factors that can affect your ROI, such as the condition of the property and the rental demand in the area.

It's important to regularly review your budget and financial projections and adjust them as needed. Keep track of your actual income and expenses and compare them to your projections to identify any discrepancies. Adjust your projections as needed to ensure that they remain realistic and aligned with your investment goals. Regularly reviewing your budget and projections can help you identify potential issues and make informed decisions about your investment strategy.

By following these steps, you can develop a budget and financial projections that will help you make informed decisions about your multi-family investing venture. Remember to remain flexible and adjust your budget and projections as needed to ensure that you're taking advantage of the best investment opportunities available. With proper planning and execution, multi-family investing can be a lucrative and rewarding venture.

It's important to note that financial projections are estimates and inherently involve uncertainty. They should be regularly reviewed and updated to reflect actual performance and changing market conditions, ensuring the business plan remains relevant and realistic.

Marketing Plan

A business plan marketing plan is a section of a comprehensive business plan that outlines the company's marketing strategies, goals, and tactics to effectively reach and engage its target market. It provides a guide for promoting the company's products or services, building brand awareness, attracting customers, and ultimately driving sales and revenue.

The marketing plan begins with a thorough analysis of the target market, including demographics, psychographics, and market trends. This analysis helps the business understand its customers' needs, preferences, and behaviors, enabling the development of targeted marketing initiatives.

Within the marketing plan, the business identifies its unique value proposition and competitive advantage. It highlights the features, benefits, and differentiation of its products or services compared to competitors, positioning the business effectively in the market.

The plan outlines the marketing strategies and tactics that the business will employ to create brand awareness, generate leads, and convert prospects into customers. It includes the channels through which the business will reach its target audience, such as digital marketing, traditional advertising, social media, public relations, direct marketing, or partnerships.

Moreover, the marketing plan addresses the pricing strategy, considering factors such as market positioning, competitive pricing, and perceived value. It outlines how the business will determine pricing models, discounts, incentives, and pricing adjustments over time.

The marketing plan also covers the customer relationship management strategy. It defines how the business will nurture and maintain relationships with customers to drive loyalty and repeat business. This may include strategies for customer retention, customer support, personalized marketing, and gathering customer feedback.

Measurement and analysis play a vital role in the marketing plan as well. The plan identifies the key performance indicators (KPIs) that will be tracked to assess the effectiveness of marketing efforts. This may include metrics such as customer acquisition cost (CAC), conversion rates, customer lifetime value (CLV), return on marketing investment (ROMI), and brand recognition.

A business plan marketing plan is a strategic document that outlines the company's marketing objectives, strategies, and tactics. It provides a projection for effectively reaching and engaging the target market, creating brand awareness, generating leads, and driving sales. The marketing plan aligns marketing activities with the overall business strategy, ensuring a focused and cohesive approach to market the products or services successfully.

Management Plan

A business plan management plan outlines the organizational structure, roles and responsibilities, and management strategies of a company. It provides a clear road-map for how the business will be managed and led to achieve its objectives and ensure operational efficiency.

The management plan typically starts with a description of the company's leadership team, including key executives, managers, and their relevant expertise and experience. It highlights the qualifications and strengths of the management team, demonstrating their ability to effectively guide the business.

The plan defines the organizational structure of the company, outlining the hierarchy, reporting relationships, and departmental divisions. It identifies the key functions within the organization, such as operations, finance, marketing, human resources, and any other relevant departments, and describes the roles and responsibilities of each position.

In addition to the organizational structure, the management plan addresses the human resources strategy. It outlines the process for recruiting, selecting, and on-boarding employees, as well as strategies for training, development, and performance management. This includes discussions on employee retention, compensation, benefits, and any relevant policies or procedures.

The plan also covers the decision-making processes and communication channels within the organization. It outlines how decisions are made, the involvement of key stakeholders, and the flow of information throughout the company. It may include strategies for fostering collaboration, promoting transparency, and ensuring effective communication at all levels.

Furthermore, the management plan addresses any potential risks or challenges that may impact the business and outlines strategies for mitigating those risks. This includes contingency plans, crisis management procedures, and business continuity strategies.

Financial management is another essential component of the management plan. It outlines the financial systems, controls, and reporting mechanisms that will be in place to ensure the effective management of the company's finances. This includes budgeting, financial analysis, cash flow management, and any relevant financial policies or procedures.

Lastly, the management plan may also address the company's growth and expansion strategies. It outlines how the management team will identify new opportunities, evaluate market trends, and make strategic decisions to drive the company's growth and achieve its long-term goals.

A business plan management plan provides a comprehensive overview of how the company will be managed and led. It addresses the organizational structure, roles and responsibilities, human resources strategies, decision-making processes, risk management, financial management, and growth strategies. The management plan ensures that the business has a solid foundation for effective leadership, efficient operations, and sustainable growth.

Risk Analysis

A business plan risk analysis section is a critical component of a comprehensive business plan that focuses on identifying, assessing, and managing potential risks and uncertainties that could impact the success and operations of a business. It provides a systematic evaluation of the potential threats and challenges the business may encounter and outlines strategies to mitigate or address them effectively.

The risk analysis section begins by identifying and categorizing various types of risks that the business may face. These risks can be internal or external, and they may arise from market dynamics, industry trends, operational processes, financial factors, legal and regulatory changes, or other external events. By categorizing risks, the business can gain a better understanding of the potential sources and nature of these risks.

Once the risks are identified, the risk analysis assesses their likelihood of occurrence and potential impact on the business. This assessment allows the business to prioritize risks based on their severity and probability, focusing on those that pose the greatest threat. The risk analysis may use qualitative or quantitative methods, such as risk matrices, probability assessments, or impact assessments, to evaluate and rank the risks.

After assessing the risks, the business develops strategies and action plans to mitigate or manage them effectively. These risk mitigation strategies may involve implementing preventive measures, developing contingency plans, diversifying suppliers or markets, investing in technology or infrastructure, securing appropriate insurance coverage, or establishing strong internal controls. The goal is to minimize the likelihood and impact of risks and ensure the business can respond effectively if they occur.

The risk analysis section also considers the potential consequences of risks on the business's financial performance, operational capabilities, reputation, and overall business objectives. It may discuss the potential financial losses, disruptions to operations, regulatory penalties, damage to brand image, or other negative impacts that could result from specific risks.

Furthermore, the risk analysis section may highlight the business's risk management team or responsible individuals who will oversee the implementation of risk mitigation strategies. It emphasizes the importance of ongoing monitoring and review of risks, as well as the need for periodic reassessment and adjustment of risk mitigation plans as the business evolves.

Including a robust risk analysis section in the business plan demonstrates the business's commitment to proactive risk management and its ability to anticipate and address potential challenges. It reassures stakeholders, such as investors, lenders, and partners, that the business has considered the risks it may face and has strategies in place to mitigate them effectively. Ultimately, a comprehensive risk analysis helps enhance the overall credibility and feasibility of the business plan.

By following these steps, you can identify target markets and potential tenants for your multi-family investing venture and develop a business plan that is aligned with their needs and preferences. Remember to remain flexible and adjust your strategy as needed to ensure that you're taking advantage of the best investment opportunities available. With proper planning and execution, multi-family investing can be a lucrative and rewarding venture.

CHAPTER SIXTEEN

DUE DILIGENCE

Due diligence is a critical step in the multi-family investing process. It involves a comprehensive investigation of the property and the surrounding area to assess the investment's risks and potential returns. Conducting due diligence helps investors make informed decisions and avoid costly mistakes. Here are some more detailed steps you can take to conduct due diligence in multi-family investing:

Property inspection, make sure you hire a professional inspector to evaluate the property's physical condition thoroughly. The inspector should examine the roof, plumbing, electrical systems, HVAC, and any other critical components of the building. The inspection will identify any issues that need to be addressed, such as maintenance, repairs, or upgrades. Review the inspection report carefully and seek clarification if you have any questions.

Conduct a thorough financial analysis that will review the property's financial statements to assess its profitability. Evaluate the property's cash flow, debt service coverage ratio, and net operating income. The financial analysis will help you determine the property's potential return on investment and whether it aligns with your investment objectives. It's essential to look at historical financial data and projections for the future.

We've already discussed market analysis. Your market analysis should cover a lot of different aspects for bot the business of investing and also specific properties that an investor is considering.

For potential investment properties, conduct a comprehensive market analysis of the surrounding area to determine rental demand and competition. Evaluate local rental market conditions, such as vacancy rates, rental rates, and employment trends. Determine whether the property is located in a desirable rental market, and whether there is sufficient demand for the type of property you are considering. This analysis will help you evaluate the potential for future cash flow and assess the long-term prospects of the investment.

Conduct a physical inspection of the property. This involves hiring a professional inspector to evaluate the condition of the property's building systems, such as electrical, plumbing, and HVAC, as well as the overall condition of the property's structure, roof, and exterior.

Additionally, you should evaluate the property's common areas, amenities, and landscaping to ensure they are well-maintained and appealing to tenants. You may also want to conduct a unit inspection of a representative sample of units to assess their condition and identify any needed repairs or upgrades.

Conduct an environmental review of the property to identify any potential hazards or liabilities. This review should include an evaluation of the property's soil, water, and air quality to ensure that it is not contaminated. If the property has an underground storage tank or other environmental concerns, consult with an environmental consultant.

Review the property's financials. This involves obtaining and analyzing financial records, including:

Review current rent rolls. A rent roll is a document that lists all current tenants, their lease terms, and their rent payments. Reviewing the rent roll can help you understand the current occupancy rate and rental income for the property.

Review operating expenses which should include all the costs associated with running the property, such as maintenance, utilities, property taxes, insurance, and property management fees. Reviewing operating expenses can help you understand the property's cash flow and profitability.

Be aware of past capital expenditures and any potential capital expenditures that may be needed. Often times owners would rather sell a property than have to pay for needed capital expenditures. Capital expenditures are large expenses that are not part of the property's day-to-day operating expenses, such as major repairs or renovations. Reviewing capital expenditures can help you understand the property's long-term maintenance and improvement needs.

Evaluate the quality of the tenants and their likelihood of renewing their leases. Review the tenant screening process to ensure that it is thorough and complies with fair housing laws. Assess the tenant retention rate to evaluate the potential for future cash flow. Determine whether there are any outstanding tenant complaints or legal issues.

Assess the property management team and their experience in managing similar properties. Evaluate the property management agreement and ensure that it aligns with your investment objectives. Review the property management company's financial statements and evaluate their fee structure.

Review legal and regulatory documents related to the property. This may include:

Order a title report and review it. A title report is a document that shows the history of ownership and any liens or encumbrances on the property. Reviewing the title report can help you identify any legal issues that could impact the property's value or your ability to acquire financing.

Contact the local county building department and find out about zoning and land use regulations for the building specifically and for the surrounding areas. Reviewing zoning and land use regulations can help you understand any restrictions on the use or development of the property.

Ask the current owner to provide copies of all current lease agreements. Reviewing lease agreements can help you understand the terms and conditions of current tenant leases, including lease expiration dates, rent amounts, and security deposit amounts.

If the property is located in an area with known environmental hazards, you may need to obtain environmental reports to make certain the property is not at risk of contamination or other environmental issues.

Hire an attorney to review all legal documents related to the property. This includes leases, contracts, and zoning regulations. The attorney should identify any potential legal issues or liabilities associated with the property, such as environmental hazards, property disputes, or outstanding liens. Review the title report to ensure that there are no title defects.

Consider financing options. This may involve obtaining pre-approval for a mortgage loan or evaluating other financing options, such as private equity or a joint venture.

When evaluating financing options, you should consider the interest rate, loan terms, and fees associated with each option. Additionally, you should consider how the financing will impact your overall investment strategy and cash flow projections.

When conducting due diligence make sure you assess potential risks. This may involve identifying potential risks related to the property's location, market, financials, physical condition, legal and regulatory issues, and management.

You should also consider how external factors, such as changes in interest rates or the local economy, could impact the property's value and cash flow projections. Evaluating potential risks can help you make an informed decision about whether to move forward with the investment and develop a risk mitigation strategy.

Evaluating market data and property information is a crucial step in making informed decisions when considering a multi-family investment. By carefully analyzing relevant data and considering potential risks and opportunities, investors can make informed decisions that align with their investment goals and strategy. It's important to work with experienced professionals and conduct a thorough assessment of the market and property data to ensure a successful investment.

Conducting due diligence on a potential multi-family investment is a critical step in the investment process. By evaluating the property's location and market, financials, physical condition, legal and regulatory issues, management, financing options, and potential risks, you can make an informed decision about whether the investment is a sound opportunity that aligns with your investment goals and strategy. Remember to work with experienced professionals, including real estate agents, inspectors, and attorneys, to ensure a thorough and accurate assessment of the property.

CHAPTER SEVENTEEN

Property Management

Managing a multi-family investment property requires a broad set of skills and expertise to ensure the property is running efficiently, tenants are satisfied, and the investment generates a consistent cash flow. Property management is critical to the success of the investment, as it includes various aspects such as maintenance, tenant screening and selection, rent collection, financial management, tenant relations, and compliance with regulations and laws.

Maintenance and repairs are essential components of property management for a multi-family investment property. Property managers must ensure that the property is in good condition to maintain its value and prevent small issues from turning into significant problems that can cost more to repair. To achieve this, a maintenance schedule should be established, and routine inspections should be conducted to identify any issues that need to be addressed. For example, property managers may establish a monthly or quarterly schedule for inspecting plumbing, electrical, HVAC systems, and common areas. Additionally, prompt repairs should be made as soon as possible to prevent further damage to the property. A system for addressing tenant maintenance requests should be established, and tenants should be informed of the process for submitting requests.

One of the most critical aspects of property management for a multi-family investment property is tenant screening and selection. A thorough screening process can help ensure that only responsible and reliable tenants are selected. This can help minimize turnover and late rent payments, which can negatively impact cash flow. A comprehensive screening process should include a credit check, criminal background check, employment verification, and rental history verification. Tenants should be required to provide references from previous landlords and provide proof of income. Property managers should also develop clear tenant selection criteria and apply them consistently to all prospective tenants.

Effective rent collection and financial management are essential components of property management for a multi-family investment property. Rent should be collected on time, and tenants who are late should be followed up with promptly. Property managers should develop a rent collection policy that outlines the consequences of late payments, such as late fees and eviction. Financial management should include maintaining accurate records of income and expenses, preparing monthly financial statements, and developing an annual budget. Additionally, property managers should work closely with property owners to ensure that the investment is meeting financial goals.

Effective tenant relations and communication are crucial components of property management for a multi-family investment property. Regular communication with tenants can help ensure that they feel heard and valued, which can lead to better retention rates. Property managers should establish an open-door policy and communicate regularly with tenants through various channels such as email, phone, and social media. Additionally, tenant concerns and complaints should be addressed promptly and respectfully. Property managers should also establish clear guidelines for tenant behavior and enforce them consistently.

Property managers must comply with various regulations and laws related to multi-family investment properties. This includes complying with local zoning laws, building codes, and fair housing regulations. Failure to comply with these laws can result in penalties, fines, and legal disputes. Property managers should stay up-to-date with any changes in laws or regulations that could impact the property. Additionally, property managers should maintain accurate and up-to-date records and ensure that the property is properly insured.

Effective property management is essential for running a successful multi-family investment property. Property managers should prioritize maintenance and repairs, tenant screening and selection, rent collection and financial management, tenant relations and communication, and compliance with regulations and laws. By doing so, they can help ensure that the property generates a consistent cash flow and meets the financial goals of the property owner. Effective property management requires attention to

Investing in multi-family real estate can be a smart financial decision, but it also comes with significant responsibilities. Managing a multi-family property can be a full-time job, requiring a wide range of skills and knowledge. One way to simplify the process and maximize your returns is by hiring a property management company.

Property management companies specialize in managing multi-family properties, and they can help you with everything from collecting rent to handling maintenance and repairs. By delegating these responsibilities to a professional company, you can free up your time to focus on other aspects of your investment, such as finding new properties to invest in, building relationships with investors, and overseeing renovations or updates.

The benefits of hiring a property management company are numerous, and they include expertise, time-saving, tenant retention, and increased profitability. Property management companies have the experience and knowledge to manage all aspects of a multi-family property, including marketing vacancies, screening tenants, rent collection, maintenance, repairs, and tenant management. They can also save you significant time by handling all the day-to-day tasks associated with managing a multi-family property. By ensuring that tenants are happy and well taken care of, a property management company can help to improve tenant retention rates, leading to less vacancy and increased profitability.

When selecting a property management company, it's important to take the time to research your options thoroughly. Look for a company with experience managing multi-family properties similar to yours and check their reputation by reading reviews and talking to references. Communication is key, so ensure the company communicates clearly and frequently with you, and compare fees from different companies to ensure you're getting a fair price. Make sure the company offers all the services you need, including maintenance, repairs, tenant management, and rent collection.

Once you've selected a property management company, it's important to establish clear expectations and communication to ensure that your investment is being managed effectively. Set clear goals for the property and communicate them to the management company. Schedule regular check-ins with the management company to stay informed about the property's performance and require regular financial reports to ensure that your investment is performing as expected. Work with the management company to establish clear tenant relations policies, including how tenant complaints will be handled, and require regular property inspections to ensure that the property is being maintained properly.

Hiring a property management company can be a valuable investment for multi-family real estate investors. By selecting the right company and working closely with them, you can ease the burden of property management and maximize your investment returns. Take the time to research your options thoroughly, and establish clear expectations and communication to ensure that your investment is being managed effectively. With the right property management company, you can enjoy the benefits of owning a multi-family property without the stress and hassle of managing it yourself.

Property management fees are one of the most important considerations when selecting a property management company. These fees can vary significantly depending on the company and the services they provide. Typically, there are three types of property management fees: flat fees, percentage-based fees, and additional fees.

Flat fees are a set amount that you pay each month or year for property management services. Flat fees are often used for smaller properties or for properties with fewer units. Percentage-based fees are based on a percentage of the property's rental income. This type of fee is often used for larger properties or properties with more units. Additional fees may be charged for specific services, such as tenant screening, maintenance, repairs, or lease renewals.

When it comes to property management fees for multi-family properties, you can expect to pay between 4% to 10% of the property's rental income. For example, if your property generates $10,000 per month in rental income, you can expect to pay between $400 and $1,000 per month for property management services. Keep in mind that additional fees may also be charged for specific services.

It's important to note that while lower fees may be tempting, they may not always provide the best value. A lower-priced property management company may not provide the same level of service as a more expensive company. It's essential to compare the services provided by different companies and determine which company offers the best value for the cost.

When negotiating property management fees, it's important to be prepared and informed. Research the standard fees for similar properties in your area to ensure that you are negotiating from a position of knowledge. You may also be able to negotiate additional services or reduced fees for long-term contracts. When negotiating fees, be clear about your expectations and the services you require. Make sure that you understand the scope of the services being provided and the associated fees. It's also essential to be prepared to walk away if you're unable to reach an agreement that works for both parties.

In addition to understanding property management fees, it's also important to consider the services provided by the property management company. Look for a company that offers a comprehensive range of services, including marketing vacancies, tenant screening, rent collection, maintenance, repairs, and tenant management. A good property management company should also have a clear understanding of the local rental market and be able to provide insights into rental rates and tenant demographics.

When working with a property management company, it's important to establish clear communication and expectations. Schedule regular check-ins to stay informed about the property's performance and require regular financial reports to ensure that your investment is performing as expected. Work with the management company to establish clear tenant relations policies, including how tenant complaints will be handled, and require regular property inspections to ensure that the property is being maintained properly.

Developing a property management plan is a critical step in managing your multi-family real estate investment. A comprehensive property management plan outlines the procedures and strategies for managing your property, from tenant relations to maintenance and repairs. A well-crafted plan can help you maximize your investment returns and ensure that your property is well-maintained and profitable.

To create an effective property management plan for your multi-family real estate investment, there are several key components that you should consider.

The first step in developing a property management plan is to assess your property. This includes evaluating the condition of the property, the current tenant base, and the local rental market. This will help you identify areas of improvement and develop strategies to maximize your investment returns.

Determine Your Objectives: Once you've assessed your property, determine your objectives for the property. Do you want to maximize rental income, improve tenant satisfaction, or increase property value? Understanding your objectives will help you develop strategies and procedures for managing the property.

Develop Strategies and Procedures: Based on your objectives, develop strategies and procedures for managing the property. This includes procedures for tenant relations, maintenance and repairs, marketing and vacancy management, financial management, and emergency procedures. Make sure that all procedures are clear, consistent, and easy to follow.

Implement and Monitor Your Plan: Once you've developed your property management plan, it's time to implement and monitor it.

Make sure that all staff and tenants are aware of the procedures outlined in the plan. Monitor the performance of the property and adjust the plan as needed to maximize your returns.

Tenant relations are a crucial component of a property management plan. This includes procedures for tenant screening, lease signing, rent collection, and addressing tenant complaints and concerns. It's important to have clear procedures in place to ensure that tenant relations are handled professionally and consistently.

Maintenance and repairs are an ongoing aspect of managing a multi-family property. A property management plan should outline procedures for conducting regular inspections, responding to maintenance requests, and handling repairs. A well-crafted maintenance plan can help ensure that your property is well-maintained and minimize the risk of costly repairs.

Marketing and vacancy management are essential for maintaining a steady stream of rental income. A property management plan should include strategies for advertising vacancies, conducting showings, and screening potential tenants. This can help ensure that your property is occupied by reliable and responsible tenants.

Financial management is an important aspect of managing a multi-family property. A property management plan should include procedures for rent collection, tracking expenses, and preparing financial reports. A well-managed financial plan can help ensure that your property is profitable and that expenses are kept under control.

Emergency procedures are critical for ensuring the safety of tenants and protecting the property in case of an emergency. A property management plan should outline procedures for responding to emergencies, such as fires, floods, or natural disasters. Having clear emergency procedures in place can help

Developing a property management plan is essential for maximizing the returns on your multi-family real estate investment. A well-crafted plan should include procedures for tenant relations, maintenance and repairs, marketing and vacancy management, financial management, and emergency procedures. To develop an effective property management plan, assess your property, determine your objectives, develop strategies and procedures, and implement and monitor your plan. By developing a comprehensive property management plan, you can ensure that your multi-family real estate investment is managed effectively and efficiently, leading to long-term success.

CHAPTER EIGHTEEN

Tenant Screening and Management

Tenant screening and management are vital aspects of effective property management for multi-family real estate investments. The process of selecting the right tenants and managing them effectively can have a significant impact on the profitability and success of your investment.

The key components of tenant screening include the application process, credit reports, background checks, and income verification. An effective tenant screening process starts with a thorough application process that collects important information about potential tenants, including their employment history, rental history, and references. Credit reports are used to gain insight into a tenant's financial history, including their ability to pay bills on time and outstanding debts. Background checks provide information about a tenant's criminal history, helping landlords to determine whether a tenant is a good fit for the community. Income verification is also critical in ensuring that a tenant can afford to pay rent and other expenses.

Once tenants are selected, effective tenant management becomes crucial. The key components of tenant management include the lease agreement, rent collection, tenant relations, and maintenance and repairs.

A comprehensive lease agreement is essential for outlining the rights and responsibilities of both the landlord and the tenant. It should include provisions for rent, utilities, maintenance, and repairs. Rent collection is also critical in maintaining positive cash flow. A clear and consistent rent collection process should be established, outlining due dates and consequences for late payments.

Establishing positive tenant relations is important for maintaining a happy and cohesive community. Procedures for addressing tenant complaints and concerns should be in place, and regular communication should be maintained. Tenants who feel heard and valued are more likely to take care of the property and renew their leases.

Regular maintenance and repairs help to keep the property in good condition and prevent costly repairs in the future. A thorough process for addressing maintenance requests should be established, including the responsibilities of the landlord and the tenant. This process should be communicated clearly to tenants to avoid any confusion or misunderstandings.

To develop an effective tenant screening and management strategy, it is important to first understand the local rental market and tenant demographics. This knowledge will help to inform the screening process and determine the most effective ways to manage tenants.

Once you have a clear understanding of your local rental market and tenant demographics, you can begin developing a tenant screening process that includes an application process, credit reports, background checks, and income verification. It is also important to establish a comprehensive lease agreement, clear rent collection process, positive tenant relations, and a maintenance and repairs process.

Regularly monitoring the effectiveness of your tenant screening and management strategy and adjusting it as needed is essential for maintaining a successful multi-family real estate investment.

In conclusion, tenant screening and management are critical aspects of effective property management for multi-family real estate investments. An effective tenant screening process, comprehensive lease agreement, clear rent collection process, positive tenant relations, and a maintenance and repairs process are essential for maximizing returns on your investment. Understanding your local rental market and tenant demographics and regularly monitoring the effectiveness of your strategy will help ensure the long-term success of your investment.

Screening potential tenants is a critical component of effective property management for multi-family real estate investments. The screening process helps landlords to identify responsible and reliable tenants who will take good care of the property and pay rent on time. It is important to develop a thorough screening process that includes several key components.

The first component of tenant screening is the application process. A comprehensive application form should be developed that collects important information, such as employment history, rental history, and references. It is important to ensure that the application form is comprehensive and that all fields are filled out completely. This information will help landlords to evaluate a potential tenant's ability to pay rent and take good care of the property.

The second component of tenant screening is reviewing credit reports. Credit reports provide insight into a tenant's financial history, including their ability to pay bills on time and outstanding debts. Reviewing a potential tenant's credit report is an important component of the screening process. It can help landlords to determine whether a tenant is likely to pay rent on time.

The third component of tenant screening is conducting background checks. Background checks provide information about a tenant's criminal history, including any previous convictions. This information can help landlords to determine whether a tenant is likely to be a good fit for the community. It is important to comply with local laws and regulations regarding background checks.

The fourth component of tenant screening is verifying income. Verifying a tenant's income helps to ensure that they can afford to pay rent and other expenses. A thorough income verification process should include employment verification and documentation of other sources of income.

The fifth component of tenant screening is conducting personal interviews. A personal interview is an important aspect of the screening process. This provides an opportunity to meet the tenant face-to-face, ask questions, and clarify any potential issues or concerns. It can also help to evaluate the tenant's character, work ethic, and other factors that may impact their ability to be a responsible and reliable tenant.

Once all of the information has been gathered during the screening process, landlords can evaluate the potential tenant and make a decision about whether to accept or reject them. It is important to document the decision and the reasons for it to avoid any potential legal issues in the future.

Developing an effective tenant screening process requires careful planning and attention to detail. It is important to understand local laws and regulations regarding tenant screening and to comply with them. In addition, landlords should be prepared to handle any potential issues that may arise during the screening process, such as incomplete application forms or discrepancies in the information provided.

Effective tenant screening helps to ensure that a multi-family property is well-maintained and profitable. By identifying responsible and reliable tenants, landlords can minimize the risk of unpaid rent, property damage, and other issues that can impact the success of the investment. Developing a thorough screening process that includes several key components is an essential step in effective property management for multi-family real estate investments.

Developing tenant leases is a crucial aspect of effective property management for multi-family real estate investments. A comprehensive and well-crafted lease agreement can help to protect the interests of both the landlord and the tenant, ensure that rent is paid on time, and establish clear expectations for maintenance and repairs.

Key Components of Tenant Leases

Rent is a critical component of the lease agreement. The lease agreement should clearly state the amount of rent, the due date, and any consequences for late payments. It should also specify any additional fees or charges, such as pet fees or late fees. It is important to be transparent and consistent in the rent collection process to avoid any confusion or misunderstandings.

The lease agreement should clearly specify the length of the lease term, whether it is a month-to-month or a fixed-term lease. This helps to establish a clear understanding of the rental period and expectations for both the landlord and the tenant.

The lease agreement should specify the amount of the security deposit and the conditions under which it will be returned to the tenant. It should also outline any deductions that may be made from the security deposit for damages or unpaid rent. This helps to protect the landlord's interests and ensure that the rental unit is well-maintained.

The lease agreement should establish the responsibilities of both the landlord and the tenant for maintenance and repairs. This includes routine maintenance, repairs, and any improvements to the property. It is important to be clear about who is responsible for which tasks to avoid any misunderstandings or disputes.

The lease agreement should specify which utilities are included in the rent and which are the responsibility of the tenant. This helps to avoid any confusion about who is responsible for paying for utilities and can help to ensure that utility bills are paid on time.

The lease agreement should specify the maximum number of occupants allowed in the rental unit and any restrictions on subletting. This helps to ensure that the rental unit is not overcrowded and that the landlord's property is protected.

Creating an Effective Lease Agreement

To create an effective lease agreement for your multi-family real estate investment, follow these steps:

Research Local Laws and Regulations. It is important to research local laws and regulations related to tenant leases to ensure that your lease agreement complies with local requirements. This helps to avoid any legal issues in the future.

Identify the key components of the lease agreement, including rent, term, security deposit, maintenance and repairs, utilities, and occupancy. This helps to ensure that all important details are included in the lease agreement.

Write the lease agreement in clear, concise language that is easy to understand. Avoid using legal jargon or complicated language that may be difficult for tenants to understand. This helps to ensure that the lease agreement is accessible to all parties involved.

Include important information, such as the address of the rental unit, the name of the landlord and tenant, and any additional fees or charges. This helps to ensure that all relevant information is included in the lease agreement.

Review and revise the lease agreement regularly to ensure that it is up-to-date and reflects

Developing tenant leases for multi-family real estate investments is an important aspect of effective property management. A well-crafted lease agreement can help to protect the interests of both the landlord and the tenant, ensure that rent is paid on time, and establish clear expectations for maintenance and repairs. The key components of a lease agreement include rent, term, security deposit, maintenance and repairs, utilities, and occupancy. By following the steps outlined in this chapter and creating an effective lease agreement, landlords can establish a positive and profitable multi-family real estate investment.

Investing in multifamily properties is a popular way to build wealth and generate passive income. However, being a landlord comes with significant responsibilities. One of the most important aspects of being a landlord is understanding tenant rights and ensuring that they are respected and upheld. Tenant rights are protected by law, and as a landlord, it is important to know these rights to avoid legal problems.

The first tenant right that landlords must understand is the right to a habitable living space. This means that landlords must maintain the property in a safe and livable condition. Landlords must provide a clean and pest-free environment, functioning plumbing, heating, and electrical systems. Additionally, landlords must ensure that the property meets building codes and other legal requirements.

The second tenant right is the right to privacy. Tenants have the right to privacy in their homes, and landlords must provide notice before entering a tenant's unit. Generally, landlords must give tenants at least 24 hours' notice before entering the property. However, landlords may enter without notice in case of an emergency.

The third tenant right is the right to quiet enjoyment. Tenants have the right to enjoy their homes without unreasonable disturbances. Landlords must ensure that other tenants or the landlord's activities do not disturb their quiet enjoyment.

The fourth tenant right is the right to a return of their security deposit. Landlords are required to return the security deposit at the end of the lease term, provided there is no damage to the property beyond normal wear and tear. If the landlord retains any portion of the deposit, they must provide an itemized list of deductions to the tenant.

Along with understanding tenant rights, landlords also have several responsibilities to uphold. One of the primary responsibilities is maintaining the property. Landlords must ensure that the property is in a safe and livable condition. They must repair any damage or wear and tear that occurs during the tenant's stay.

Another landlord responsibility is providing essential services. Landlords must provide tenants with essential services such as heat, hot water, and electricity. Failure to provide these services can lead to legal issues and possible eviction.

Landlords must also ensure fair housing practices. This means that landlords cannot discriminate against tenants based on protected classes such as race, gender, religion, or national origin. Landlords must provide equal opportunities to all potential tenants.

Handling security deposits is also a responsibility of landlords. Landlords must handle security deposits according to state laws. This includes providing tenants with a written statement of any deductions taken from the deposit. If a landlord fails to handle the security deposit properly, it can lead to legal issues.

Lastly, landlords must provide notice before entering the unit or making changes to the rental agreement. This is a requirement by law and helps to protect the tenant's privacy.

In addition to understanding tenant rights and landlord

responsibilities, landlords can follow best practices to create a positive relationship with tenants. Having a clear and detailed lease agreement can help outline the responsibilities of both the landlord and the tenant. Conducting regular property inspections can help identify any maintenance issues before they become larger problems. Responding promptly to tenant requests and providing open communication can help prevent misunderstandings and build a positive relationship.

Understanding tenant rights and landlord responsibilities is essential for any landlord who wants to succeed in the multifamily investment property business. By upholding these rights and responsibilities, landlords can create a safe and comfortable living environment for tenants and build a profitable investment portfolio. It is important for landlords to educate themselves on tenant rights and regularly review their practices to ensure compliance with the law.

CHAPTER NINETEEN

Maintenance and Repairs

Multi-family real estate investments can be a lucrative venture for property investors. However, they also come with a unique set of challenges that require careful consideration, including maintenance and repairs. Proper maintenance and repairs are crucial for keeping the property in good condition and attracting tenants. In this chapter, we will explore the importance of maintenance and repairs in multi-family real estate investments and why they are essential for ensuring the property's profitability.

Regular maintenance involves the routine inspection and repair of a building's structural and mechanical systems. The goal of regular maintenance is to identify and fix small issues before they become significant problems, which can help extend the lifespan of the building and its components. Regular maintenance can include:

HVAC System Maintenance, heating, ventilation, and air conditioning (HVAC) systems play a critical role in ensuring tenants' comfort and maintaining a healthy indoor environment. Regular HVAC system maintenance can help prevent breakdowns, improve energy efficiency, and extend the system's lifespan.

Plumbing Maintenance, plumbing issues such as leaks, clogs, and backups can cause significant damage to a property. Regular inspections and maintenance of plumbing systems can help identify and fix issues before they escalate.

Electrical System Maintenance, electrical systems can be hazardous if not maintained properly. Regular inspections and maintenance of electrical systems can help prevent electrical hazards, ensure equipment and appliances function correctly, and reduce the risk of electrical fires.

Exterior Maintenance, the exterior of a property is just as important as the interior. Regular inspections and maintenance of the roof, gutters, siding, and other exterior components can help prevent damage from water infiltration, pests, and harsh weather conditions.

Preventive maintenance involves the implementation of a regular maintenance schedule to help reduce the likelihood of future maintenance and repair costs. Preventive maintenance can include:

Regular inspections of the property can help identify potential issues before they become significant problems. These inspections can be conducted by property managers, maintenance staff, or professional inspectors.

Regular cleaning of the property can help prevent the buildup of dirt, debris, and other materials that can damage the property's systems and components.

Proper landscaping can help prevent soil erosion, drainage problems, and other issues that can damage the property.

Repairs are necessary when a system or component of a multi-family property breaks down or is damaged. Repairs can range from minor to major and can include:

Plumbing repairs can include fixing leaks, clogs, and broken pipes.

Electrical repairs can include fixing faulty wiring, replacing outlets, and repairing lighting fixtures.

HVAC repairs can include fixing broken air conditioning units, replacing heating elements, and repairing ductwork.

Exterior repairs can include fixing damaged roofs, siding, and gutters.

Budgeting for maintenance and repairs is essential for multi-family real estate investments. Property owners should set aside funds for regular maintenance and emergency repairs to ensure that the property remains in good condition and attract tenants. A good rule of thumb is to set aside 1% to 2% of the property's value annually for maintenance and repairs. It is also important to keep track of expenses to identify any areas where cost savings can be realized.

Maintenance and repairs are critical for multi-family real estate investments. Regular maintenance and preventive maintenance can help reduce the likelihood of costly repairs, while repairs can keep the property in good condition and attract tenants. Proper budgeting for maintenance and repairs can help ensure that the property remains a profitable investment for years to come.

Multi-family real estate investments require careful maintenance to ensure the property's longevity and profitability. A comprehensive maintenance plan can help prevent costly repairs, minimize downtime, and keep tenants happy. In this chapter, we will explore how to develop a maintenance plan for multi-family real estate investments, with an emphasis on detailed planning and execution.

The first step in developing a maintenance plan is to assess the property's maintenance needs. This requires a thorough inspection of the property, including its structural and mechanical systems. The inspection should identify any existing issues, potential problem areas, and maintenance requirements for each system and component of the property. This assessment will help determine the types of maintenance tasks required and how often they should be performed. It is essential to take a holistic approach and evaluate the property's condition in its entirety.

Once the maintenance needs have been assessed, the next step is to establish maintenance goals. These goals should align with the property's overall business strategy and consider the needs of the tenants. The goals should include prioritizing safety, maintaining the property's value, and enhancing the tenant experience. Clear goals help ensure that maintenance efforts are focused, effective, and in line with the property's objectives.

After establishing maintenance goals, the next step is to create a maintenance schedule. This schedule should identify the types of maintenance tasks required, how often they should be performed, and who will be responsible for performing them. The schedule should be flexible to accommodate unexpected maintenance needs, such as emergency repairs or tenant requests. A well-designed schedule helps ensure that maintenance tasks are performed regularly and in a timely manner.

Assigning responsibilities is a critical step in developing a maintenance plan. Clear roles and responsibilities ensure that everyone knows what tasks they are responsible for and when they need to be completed. Property managers, maintenance staff, and outside contractors may all play a role in the maintenance plan. Defining responsibilities and holding individuals accountable for their tasks helps ensure that maintenance tasks are performed consistently and to the highest standards.

Creating a budget is another important step in developing a maintenance plan. The budget should be based on the property's maintenance needs and goals and should include a contingency fund for unexpected maintenance expenses. Property owners should consider the cost of preventative maintenance compared to the cost of emergency repairs when creating their budget. A well-planned budget helps ensure that adequate funds are available to cover the property's maintenance needs.

Once the maintenance plan has been developed, it should be documented to ensure that everyone understands the plan's objectives, responsibilities, and schedule. The documentation should include the maintenance schedule, budget, responsibilities, and any relevant procedures. Documentation ensures that the maintenance plan is communicated effectively and helps ensure that the plan is followed consistently.

Once the maintenance plan is developed and documented, it is time to implement it. Property owners and managers must work closely with the maintenance staff and contractors to ensure that the maintenance plan is executed effectively. Regular monitoring of the maintenance plan is necessary to ensure that it remains effective and relevant. Adjustments may be necessary based on changing circumstances, such as tenant turnover or changes in market conditions.

Developing a maintenance plan is essential for multi-family real estate investments. A well-designed plan helps ensure that maintenance tasks are performed regularly and in a timely manner, preventing costly repairs and minimizing downtime. When developing a maintenance plan, property owners should assess the property's maintenance needs, establish maintenance goals, create a maintenance schedule, assign responsibilities, create a budget, document the plan, implement it, and monitor its effectiveness.

Owning and managing a multi-family property can be a lucrative investment opportunity, but it also requires careful financial planning and budgeting. One of the most important aspects of managing a multi-family property is budgeting for repairs and improvements. In this chapter, we will discuss the key considerations for budgeting for repairs and improvements for multi-family property investments, including assessing the property's condition, developing a maintenance plan, estimating costs, prioritizing repairs and improvements, and creating a reserve fund.

The first step in budgeting for repairs and improvements is to assess the condition of the property. This includes conducting a thorough inspection of the building, identifying any existing issues or potential problems, and determining the overall age and condition of the property. During the inspection, it's important to check for issues such as leaks, cracks, mold, pest infestations, and structural problems. Additionally, it's important to assess the condition of the property's major systems, such as the HVAC system, plumbing, electrical, and roofing. Based on this assessment, you can develop a plan for repairs and improvements, prioritize the work that needs to be done, and estimate the associated costs.

Once you have assessed the property's condition, the next step is to develop a maintenance plan. This plan should include a schedule for regular maintenance tasks, such as cleaning, painting, and landscaping, as well as a plan for addressing larger repairs and improvements over time. By developing a maintenance plan, you can ensure that you are proactively addressing maintenance needs and avoiding costly emergency repairs. Additionally, having a well-maintained property can help attract and retain tenants, which can increase your property's value and generate higher rental income.

When budgeting for repairs and improvements, it is important to estimate the costs associated with each project. This includes not only the cost of materials and labor, but also any permits or inspections that may be required. It's a good idea to obtain multiple quotes from contractors and vendors to ensure that you are getting a fair price for the work that needs to be done. Additionally, it's important to budget for unexpected costs or contingencies, such as the discovery of additional damage during the repair process.

When budgeting for repairs and improvements, it is important to prioritize the work that needs to be done. This includes addressing any urgent repairs or safety issues first, such as broken windows or electrical problems. Once these urgent repairs are taken care of, you can then focus on making improvements that will increase the property's value or improve the quality of life for your tenants, such as updating appliances or adding amenities like a fitness center or pool. Additionally, it's important to consider the ROI (return on investment) of each repair or improvement project. For example, investing in energy-efficient upgrades may result in lower utility bills and increased property value, making it a worthwhile investment.

To ensure that you have sufficient funds available for repairs and improvements, it is a good idea to create a reserve fund. This fund should be set aside specifically for maintenance and repairs, and should be regularly maintained to ensure that you have the necessary funds available when needed. Ideally, your reserve fund should be sufficient to cover at least six months of operating expenses. By having a reserve fund, you can avoid having to dip into your personal funds or take out loans to cover unexpected repairs or maintenance needs. Reserve funds for maintenance should be a line item cost. By contributing to your maintenance reserve fund as a cost, you don't pay taxes on the funds that go into your reserve. When you use funds from your reserve they are   non taxed. Investors who pay for maintenance and capital improvements from their own pocket are paying for them with money they've already paid taxes on. That isn't getting the most for your money.

Budgeting for repairs and improvements is a critical aspect of managing a multi-family property investment. By assessing the property's condition, developing a maintenance plan, estimating costs, prioritizing repairs and improvements, and creating a reserve fund, you can ensure that you are proactively managing maintenance needs and avoiding costly emergency repairs. With careful planning and budgeting, you can maximize the return on your investment while providing a safe and comfortable living environment for your tenants.

As a landlord, you are responsible for ensuring that your multi-family investment property is safe, habitable, and well-maintained. This includes addressing any necessary repairs in a timely manner. By understanding your landlord responsibilities for repairs, you can protect your investment, ensure the safety and well-being of your tenants, and avoid potential legal issues.

One of the most important landlord responsibilities when it comes to repairs is providing a safe and habitable living space for your tenants. This means that you must maintain the property in a condition that is suitable for human habitation, including ensuring that all essential utilities and services are in working order. You are also responsible for addressing any health and safety concerns that may arise, such as mold or pest infestations.

When it comes to repairs, there are several key areas that you need to be aware of as a landlord. These include structural repairs, plumbing and electrical repairs, heating and cooling repairs, and appliance repairs.

Structural repairs are among the most important repairs that you may need to address as a landlord. You must ensure that the structure of your property is sound and secure. This includes fixing any issues with the foundation, walls, roof, and other structural components. Failure to address structural issues can lead to serious safety hazards and can also compromise the integrity of your investment property.

Plumbing and electrical repairs are also essential to maintaining the safety and comfort of your tenants. You must ensure that the plumbing and electrical systems in your property are in good working order. This includes fixing any leaks, repairing broken pipes, and addressing any electrical issues. These repairs can help prevent water damage, electrical hazards, and other potentially dangerous situations.

Heating and cooling repairs are also important to address in a timely manner. You are responsible for ensuring that the heating and cooling systems in your property are functioning properly. This includes repairing or replacing HVAC systems as needed. Failure to address heating and cooling issues can lead to uncomfortable living conditions and can even be a health hazard in extreme temperatures.

If you provide appliances in your rental units, such as refrigerators, stoves, and washers and dryers, you are responsible for repairing or replacing them if they break down. This is an important responsibility as appliances that are not in good working order can lead to tenant dissatisfaction and can also compromise the safety of your property.

In addition to addressing repairs promptly, it is important to communicate effectively with your tenants about any maintenance issues. You should have a clear process in place for tenants to report any maintenance issues, and you should respond to these reports promptly. You should also communicate with your tenants about any repairs that need to be made and provide them with a timeline for when the repairs will be completed.

Keeping thorough records of all maintenance and repairs is also essential as a landlord. This can help protect you in the event of any disputes with tenants and can also help you track the overall condition of your property. By keeping detailed records, you can identify any recurring issues and address them proactively, rather than waiting for them to become major problems.

Understanding your landlord responsibilities for repairs is essential for the success of your multi-family investment property. By prioritizing maintenance and repairs, communicating effectively with your tenants, and keeping thorough records, you can ensure that your property remains in good condition and that your tenants are happy and satisfied with their living arrangements. Failure to address repairs in a timely manner can lead to safety hazards, tenant dissatisfaction, and potentially costly legal issues. As a responsible landlord, it is essential that you take your repair responsibilities seriously and address any issues promptly and effectively.

CHAPTER TWENTY

Risk Management

As a real estate investor, you'll find that owning and managing multi-family investment properties can be an incredibly lucrative venture. However, with any investment comes risks. In order to ensure the long-term success of your investment, it is crucial to develop a comprehensive risk management plan. This chapter will provide an overview of risk management for multi-family investment properties, including the key risks that you may face and strategies for mitigating those risks.

Before you can develop a risk management plan, it is important to identify the risks that you may face as a landlord of a multi-family investment property. This chapter will provide an overview of the key risks that you may encounter, including risks related to property damage, tenant issues, legal liabilities, and financial risks.

Property damage is a common risk that landlords of multi-family investment properties may face. This chapter will provide an overview of strategies for mitigating property damage risks, including regular property inspections, preventative maintenance, and insurance coverage.

Tenant issues can also pose a significant risk to landlords of multi-family investment properties. This chapter will explore strategies for mitigating tenant issues, including thorough tenant screening, effective communication, and dispute resolution procedures.

Legal liabilities can be a major risk for landlords of multi-family investment properties. This chapter will discuss strategies for mitigating legal liabilities, including compliance with fair housing laws, proper record keeping, and insurance coverage.

Financial risks can also be a concern for landlords of multi-family investment properties. This chapter will explore strategies for mitigating financial risks, including budgeting and cash flow management, diversification of investments, and contingency planning.

With an understanding of the key risks and strategies for mitigating those risks, it is now possible to develop a comprehensive risk management plan. This chapter will provide an overview of the components of a successful risk management plan, including risk assessment, risk mitigation strategies, and ongoing monitoring and evaluation.

Once a risk management plan has been developed, it is important to implement it effectively. This chapter will explore strategies for implementing a risk management plan, including communication with tenants and staff, regular monitoring and evaluation, and ongoing training and development.

Risk management is an ongoing process that requires regular evaluation and updating. This chapter will explore strategies for evaluating and updating a risk management plan, including the use of performance metrics and feedback from tenants and staff.

Effective risk management is essential for the long-term success of multi-family investment properties. By identifying and mitigating key risks, developing a comprehensive risk management plan, and implementing ongoing monitoring and evaluation, landlords can protect their investment and ensure the safety and satisfaction of their tenants.

Investing in multi-family real estate can be a lucrative venture, but it is not without risks. As a real estate investor, it is essential to identify potential risks that may impact your investment. By doing so, you can take proactive steps to mitigate these risks and protect your investment. This chapter will explore some of the potential risks associated with multi-family real estate investment and provide strategies for managing them.

One of the most common risks associated with multi-family real estate investment is property damage. This can be caused by natural disasters such as floods, fires, and earthquakes, as well as by human actions such as vandalism or neglect. Property damage can be expensive to repair and can result in lost rental income while the property is being repaired.

To mitigate the risk of property damage, it is important to invest in a property that is located in a low-risk area, such as an area with low flood or fire risk. It is also important to regularly inspect the property for any potential issues and to address any repairs promptly. Additionally, investing in comprehensive property insurance coverage can help mitigate the financial impact of property damage.

Tenant issues can also be a potential risk for multi-family real estate investors. These issues can include non-payment of rent, property damage caused by tenants, and legal disputes with tenants. These issues can result in lost rental income, legal fees, and damage to the property.

To mitigate the risk of tenant issues, it is important to conduct thorough tenant screening before leasing a property. This screening should include a credit check, criminal background check, and references from previous landlords. Additionally, effective communication with tenants can help prevent potential disputes and address issues promptly when they do arise.

Legal liabilities are another potential risk for multi-family real estate investors. These can include lawsuits from tenants, non-compliance with fair housing laws, and building code violations. Legal liabilities can result in significant financial losses and can also damage the reputation of the property and the investor.

To mitigate the risk of legal liabilities, it is important to stay up-to-date on all relevant laws and regulations, such as fair housing laws and building codes. Additionally, maintaining thorough documentation and records can help protect investors in the event of a legal dispute.

Financial risks are another potential risk for multi-family real estate investors. These risks can include changes in market conditions, rising interest rates, and changes in tax laws. Financial risks can impact the profitability of the investment and can result in financial losses.

To mitigate financial risks, it is important to conduct thorough market research before investing in a property. This research should include an analysis of market conditions, interest rates, and tax laws. Additionally, it is important to maintain adequate cash reserves and to diversify investments to spread risk across multiple properties.

Identifying potential risks associated with multi-family real estate investment is an essential step in protecting your investment. By understanding the potential risks and developing strategies for managing them, investors can mitigate the financial impact of these risks and protect their investment. Regular property inspections, effective communication with tenants, compliance with relevant laws and regulations, and market research are all important tools for managing potential risks associated with multi-family real estate investment.

Effective risk management is essential for the long-term success of multi-family investment properties. Developing a comprehensive risk management plan can help investors identify and mitigate potential risks, protect their investment, and ensure the safety and satisfaction of their tenants. This chapter will provide an overview of the key components of a risk management plan for multi-family investment properties, including risk assessment, risk mitigation strategies, and ongoing monitoring and evaluation.

The first step in developing a risk management plan for multi-family investment properties is to conduct a risk assessment. This assessment should include an evaluation of potential risks, such as property damage, tenant issues, legal liabilities, and financial risks. Investors should also evaluate the likelihood and potential impact of each risk.

Once potential risks have been identified, investors can develop strategies for mitigating these risks. These strategies should be tailored to the specific risks and should take into account the likelihood and potential impact of each risk.

The next step in developing a risk management plan is to develop risk mitigation strategies. These strategies should be designed to reduce the likelihood and potential impact of each identified risk.

For example, to mitigate the risk of property damage, investors may implement regular property inspections and maintenance procedures. To mitigate the risk of tenant issues, investors may develop effective communication strategies and dispute resolution procedures. To mitigate the risk of legal liabilities, investors may develop compliance protocols and maintain thorough documentation and records. To mitigate financial risks, investors may diversify investments and maintain adequate cash reserves.

Once a risk management plan has been developed and implemented, it is important to monitor and evaluate the effectiveness of the plan on an ongoing basis. This evaluation should include an analysis of the effectiveness of risk mitigation strategies, as well as an assessment of any new or emerging risks.

Ongoing monitoring and evaluation can help investors identify areas where the risk management plan can be improved and can also help investors stay up-to-date on changes in market conditions, legal requirements, and other factors that may impact their investment.

Developing a comprehensive risk management plan is essential for the long-term success of multi-family investment properties. By conducting a risk assessment, developing tailored risk mitigation strategies, and conducting ongoing monitoring and evaluation, investors can identify and mitigate potential risks, protect their investment, and ensure the safety and satisfaction of their tenants. Regular communication with tenants and staff, implementation of best practices for property management, and proactive risk management strategies can all contribute to the success of multi-family investment properties.

Effective risk management is essential for the long-term success of multi-family investment properties. Developing a comprehensive risk management plan can help investors identify and mitigate potential risks, protect their investment, and ensure the safety and satisfaction of their tenants. This chapter will provide an overview of the key components of a risk management plan for multi-family investment properties, including risk assessment, risk mitigation strategies, and ongoing monitoring and evaluation.

The first step in developing a risk management plan for multi-family investment properties is to conduct a risk assessment. This assessment should include an evaluation of potential risks, such as property damage, tenant issues, legal liabilities, and financial risks. Investors should also evaluate the likelihood and potential impact of each risk.

Once potential risks have been identified, investors can develop strategies for mitigating these risks. These strategies should be tailored to the specific risks and should take into account the likelihood and potential impact of each risk.

The next step in developing a risk management plan is to develop risk mitigation strategies. These strategies should be designed to reduce the likelihood and potential impact of each identified risk.

For example, to mitigate the risk of property damage, investors may implement regular property inspections and maintenance procedures. To mitigate the risk of tenant issues, investors may develop effective communication strategies and dispute resolution procedures. To mitigate the risk of legal liabilities, investors may develop compliance protocols and maintain thorough documentation and records. To mitigate financial risks, investors may diversify investments and maintain adequate cash reserves.

Once a risk management plan has been developed and implemented, it is important to monitor and evaluate the effectiveness of the plan on an ongoing basis. This evaluation should include an analysis of the effectiveness of risk mitigation strategies, as well as an assessment of any new or emerging risks.

Ongoing monitoring and evaluation can help investors identify areas where the risk management plan can be improved and can also help investors stay up-to-date on changes in market conditions, legal requirements, and other factors that may impact their investment.

Developing a comprehensive risk management plan is essential for the long-term success of multi-family investment properties. By conducting a risk assessment, developing tailored risk mitigation strategies, and conducting ongoing monitoring and evaluation, investors can identify and mitigate potential risks, protect their investment, and ensure the safety and satisfaction of their tenants. Regular communication with tenants and staff, implementation of best practices for property management, and proactive risk management strategies can all contribute to the success of multi-family investment properties.

Insurance coverage is an important aspect of risk management for multi-family real estate investments. Understanding insurance requirements and options can help investors protect their investment and mitigate potential risks. This chapter will provide an overview of insurance requirements and options for multi-family real estate investments, including property insurance, liability insurance, and flood insurance.

Property insurance is a type of insurance coverage that protects against damage to the physical structure of a property. This can include damage caused by natural disasters, such as fires and floods, as well as damage caused by human actions, such as vandalism or theft.

Most lenders require that multi-family real estate investors have property insurance coverage in place as a condition of the loan. Property insurance typically covers the cost of repairs or rebuilding of the property in the event of damage, as well as loss of rental income during the repair period.

When selecting a property insurance policy, it is important to ensure that the policy provides adequate coverage for the specific risks associated with the property. This may include coverage for damage caused by natural disasters, damage caused by tenants, and other potential risks.

Liability insurance is a type of insurance coverage that protects against lawsuits or claims made against the property owner or manager. This can include claims for injuries sustained by tenants or visitors to the property, as well as claims related to property damage caused by the owner or manager.

Most lenders require that multi-family real estate investors have liability insurance coverage in place as a condition of the loan. Liability insurance typically covers the cost of legal fees and damages awarded in the event of a lawsuit or claim.

When selecting a liability insurance policy, it is important to ensure that the policy provides adequate coverage for the specific risks associated with the property. This may include coverage for injuries sustained by tenants or visitors, as well as property damage caused by the owner or manager.

Flood insurance is a type of insurance coverage that protects against damage caused by floods. This can be an important consideration for multi-family real estate investments located in flood-prone areas.

While flood insurance is not typically required by lenders, it may be a requirement of local or federal regulations. Additionally, investing in flood insurance can help mitigate the financial impact of flood-related damage to the property.

When selecting a flood insurance policy, it is important to ensure that the policy provides adequate coverage for the specific risks associated with the property. This may include coverage for damage caused by flash floods, river flooding, or storm surges.

Understanding insurance requirements and options is an important aspect of risk management for multi-family real estate investments. Property insurance, liability insurance, and flood insurance are all important types of insurance coverage that can help protect investors from potential financial losses. When selecting insurance policies, it is important to ensure that the policies provide adequate coverage for the specific risks associated with the property. Regularly reviewing and updating insurance coverage can help ensure that investors are adequately protected and can help mitigate potential risks.

CHAPTER TWENTY ONE

Tax Strategies

Effective tax planning is an important aspect of multi-family real estate investment. By understanding tax strategies and taking advantage of tax incentives, investors can maximize their profits and reduce their tax liability. This chapter will provide an overview of tax strategies for multi-family investment properties, including depreciation, cost segregation, and 1031 exchanges.

Depreciation is a tax deduction that allows investors to deduct a portion of the cost of a property over time. This deduction can help reduce the taxable income of the property and can result in lower tax liability for the investor.

The depreciation deduction is calculated based on the value of the property and the length of time it is expected to be in service. In general, residential rental properties are depreciated over 27.5 years, while commercial properties are depreciated over 39 years.

It is important to note that while depreciation can reduce tax liability, it also reduces the basis of the property. This can result in higher capital gains taxes when the property is eventually sold.

Cost segregation is a tax planning strategy that allows investors to accelerate depreciation and reduce tax liability. This strategy involves separating the components of a property into different asset classes, each with a different depreciation period.

For example, a cost segregation analysis may identify certain components of a property that can be classified as personal property and depreciated over a shorter period of time than the overall property. This can result in a larger depreciation deduction and lower tax liability for the investor.

A 1031 exchange is a tax-deferred exchange of like-kind properties. This strategy allows investors to sell a property and reinvest the proceeds in a new property without paying capital gains taxes on the sale.

To qualify for a 1031 exchange, the properties must be considered like-kind, meaning they must be of the same nature or character, such as both being rental properties. Additionally, the exchange must be completed within a certain time-frame and certain other requirements must be met.

Effective tax planning is an important aspect of multi-family real estate investment. By taking advantage of tax strategies such as depreciation, cost segregation, and 1031 exchanges, investors can maximize their profits and reduce their tax liability. It is important to work with a qualified tax professional when developing tax strategies for multi-family investment properties to ensure compliance with all relevant tax laws and regulations.

Effective tax planning is essential for maximizing profits and minimizing expenses associated with multi-family real estate investments. By understanding and implementing the right tax strategies, investors can reduce their tax liability, increase cash flow, and enhance the overall return on their investment. This chapter will provide a more detailed overview of some of the key tax strategies available to multi-family real estate investors, including depreciation, cost segregation, 1031 exchanges, and other potential tax deductions.

Depreciation is an essential tax strategy for real estate investors, as it allows them to deduct a portion of the cost of a property over its useful life. The depreciation deduction can help to reduce taxable income, which in turn can help to minimize the amount of tax owed.

Depreciation is typically calculated based on the cost of the property, the value of the land, and the estimated useful life of the property. In general, the useful life of residential rental property is 27.5 years, while commercial property is depreciated over a 39-year period.

It is important to note that while depreciation can reduce tax liability, it can also reduce the basis of the property, which can increase capital gains taxes when the property is eventually sold.

In addition to depreciation, cost segregation, and 1031 exchanges, there are several other potential tax deductions that multi-family real estate investors can take advantage of. These may include:

Interest deductions, investors can deduct the interest paid on mortgages and other loans used to finance the property.

Operating expenses, expenses associated with the day-to-day operations of the property, such as property management fees, maintenance expenses, and utilities, can be deducted.

Home office deduction, if the investor has a home office that is exclusively used for managing the property, they may be able to deduct a portion of their home-related expenses.

It is important to work with a qualified tax professional to ensure that all potential tax deductions are identified and properly documented.

Effective tax planning is essential for maximizing profits and minimizing expenses associated with multi-family real estate investments. By understanding and implementing the right tax strategies, investors can reduce their tax liability, increase cash flow, and enhance the overall return on their investment. In addition to depreciation, cost segregation, and 1031 exchanges, other potential tax deductions may also be available to investors. It is important to work

Multi-family real estate investments can provide a stable income stream, tax benefits, and long-term appreciation potential. However, as with any investment, understanding the tax implications is critical to maximizing returns and minimizing expenses. In this chapter, we will provide a more in-depth analysis of the tax implications associated with investing in multi-family real estate, including taxes on rental income, capital gains taxes, and other relevant tax considerations.

One of the most significant tax implications of investing in multi-family real estate is the taxation of rental income. Rental income, that is profit after all of an investors costs and expenses for a property is generally considered taxable income and is subject to federal and state income taxes. In addition, investors may also be subject to self-employment taxes, which are designed to cover Social Security and Medicare taxes for self-employed individuals.

It is important to note that rental income may be offset by certain tax deductions, such as depreciation, mortgage interest, and property taxes. Depreciation is a particularly important deduction for real estate investors, as it allows them to recover the cost of the property over time.

Mortgage interest and property taxes are also deductible, subject to certain limitations. It is important to work with a qualified tax professional to ensure that all relevant deductions are identified and properly documented.

Capital gains taxes are another important tax consideration for multi-family real estate investors. Capital gains taxes are levied on the profit made from the sale of an investment property, and can have a significant impact on the overall profitability of the investment.

The amount of capital gains tax owed is generally calculated by subtracting the basis of the property from the sales price of the property. The basis of the property includes the original purchase price, as well as any improvements or capital expenses made over the course of ownership.

Investors may be able to reduce their capital gains tax liability by taking advantage of tax strategies such as 1031 exchanges, which allow them to defer taxes by reinvesting the proceeds in a like-kind property, placing properties into trust, purchasing properties as corporations and other strategies.

In addition to rental income taxes and capital gains taxes, there are several other tax considerations that multi-family real estate investors should be aware of. These may include:

Property taxes are generally assessed by local governments and are based on the assessed value of the property. Property taxes can have a significant impact on the overall profitability of the investment.

In addition to federal taxes, multi-family real estate investors may also be subject to state and local taxes, such as sales taxes, use taxes, and transfer taxes.

Passive activity loss rules. The IRS has established passive activity loss rules that limit the ability of investors to deduct losses associated with passive activities, such as rental real estate. Investors should be aware of these rules and work with a qualified tax professional to develop a tax strategy that maximizes deductions while remaining in compliance with IRS regulations.

Depreciation recapture is when a property is sold, any depreciation claimed during ownership must be "recaptured" and taxed at a higher rate than capital gains taxes. It is important to plan for this recapture when developing a tax strategy.

Understanding the tax implications of investing in multi-family real estate is essential for maximizing profits and minimizing expenses associated with the investment. Taxes on rental income, capital gains taxes, and other relevant tax considerations can have a significant impact on the overall profitability of the investment.

It is important to work with a qualified tax professional to develop a tax strategy that takes into account all relevant tax considerations and maximizes deductions while remaining in compliance with IRS regulations. Regularly reviewing and updating tax strategies can help ensure that investors are maximizing the profitability of their investment and minimizing their tax liability. With proper planning, multi-family real estate investing

Identifying tax deductions and credits is a crucial part of maximizing the profitability of multi-family real estate investments. Tax deductions and credits can help to significantly reduce tax liability and increase cash flow, which can enhance the overall return on investment. In this chapter, we will provide a more detailed analysis of some of the most common tax deductions and credits available to multi-family real estate investors.

Depreciation is one of the most important tax deductions available to real estate investors. It allows investors to deduct a portion of the cost of a property over its useful life. This deduction can significantly reduce taxable income and tax liability.

The amount of depreciation that can be claimed is calculated based on the cost of the property, the value of the land, and the estimated useful life of the property. Residential rental properties are generally depreciated over 27.5 years, while commercial properties are depreciated over 39 years.

It is important to note that while depreciation can reduce tax liability, it also reduces the basis of the property, which can result in higher capital gains taxes when the property is sold.

Mortgage interest is another important tax deduction available to multi-family real estate investors. Investors can deduct the interest paid on mortgages used to finance the property. This deduction can significantly reduce taxable income and tax liability.

The deduction for mortgage interest is subject to certain limitations, such as a cap on the amount of mortgage debt that is eligible for the deduction. Investors should work with a qualified tax professional to ensure that they are taking full advantage of this deduction while remaining in compliance with IRS regulations.

Repairs and maintenance expenses can also be deducted from taxable income. These expenses include any necessary repairs or improvements made to the property to keep it in good condition.

It is important to note that expenses that improve the property beyond its original condition, such as major renovations or additions, may be considered capital expenses and subject to different tax treatment.

Property taxes are another important tax deduction available to multi-family real estate investors. Property taxes are generally assessed by local governments and are based on the assessed value of the property.

Property taxes can have a significant impact on the overall profitability of the investment, and it is important for investors to properly document and deduct these expenses on their tax returns.

Investors who make energy-efficient improvements to their properties may be eligible for tax credits. These tax credits can be substantial and can help offset the cost of the improvements.

Examples of energy-efficient improvements include the installation of energy-efficient windows, doors, and insulation, as well as the installation of solar panels and other renewable energy systems.

The Section 179 deduction allows business owners to deduct the full cost of certain qualifying equipment or property in the year it is purchased and placed into service, rather than depreciating the cost over time. This deduction can be particularly useful for multi-family real estate investors who are purchasing equipment for their properties, such as appliances, HVAC systems, and security systems.

It is important to work with a qualified tax professional to determine which items are eligible for the Section 179 deduction and to properly document and deduct these expenses on tax returns.

Identifying tax deductions and credits is an essential part of maximizing the profitability of multi-family real estate investments. Depreciation, mortgage interest, repairs and maintenance expenses, property taxes, energy-efficiency tax credits, and the Section 179 deduction are just a few examples of the tax deductions and credits available to investors.

It is important to work with a qualified tax professional to ensure that all relevant tax deductions and credits are identified and properly documented. Regularly reviewing for changes in tax law and requirements as well as changes in your own circumstances that might affect your own tax situation.

Multi-family real estate investments come with complex tax implications, making it essential for investors to work with a qualified tax professional. A tax professional can help investors develop a tax strategy that maximizes profitability and minimizes tax liability while ensuring compliance with IRS regulations. In this chapter, we will provide a more in-depth analysis of the benefits of working with a tax professional and the qualities to look for in a tax professional.

There are several benefits to working with a tax professional when investing in multi-family real estate. These benefits include:

A tax professional can help identify all relevant deductions and credits, including those that may be overlooked by less experienced investors helping you to maximize investments..

A tax professional can ensure that all tax strategies are in compliance with IRS regulations, minimizing the risk of costly penalties and fines and keeping you in compliance with IRS codes and requirements..

A tax professional can develop a tax strategy that is tailored to the specific needs and goals of the investor, maximizing profitability and minimizing tax liability.

A tax professional can help investors plan for future tax obligations, such as capital gains taxes and depreciation recapture, ensuring that they are properly accounted for in the investment strategy.

Working with a tax professional can significantly reduce the workload and stress associated with tax preparation and planning, allowing investors to focus on other aspects of their investment portfolio.

When selecting a tax professional to work with, there are several qualities to consider. These include:

Look for a tax professional with experience working with real estate investors and a deep understanding of the tax implications of multi-family real estate investments.

Make sure the tax professional is qualified to provide tax advice, such as holding a Certified Public Accountant (CPA) license or a tax attorney license.

A good tax professional should be able to communicate complex tax concepts in a way that is easy for investors to understand. Look for someone who is responsive and willing to answer questions.

Make sure to discuss the tax professional's fees upfront, including any fees for additional services or consultations. It is also important to ensure that the fees are reasonable and in line with industry standards.

Look for a tax professional who is available throughout the year, not just during tax season. This will ensure that the investor has access to support and guidance when needed.

Once a tax professional has been selected, it is important to establish a productive working relationship. Some tips for working effectively with a tax professional include:

Provide the tax professional with accurate and complete records, including receipts, invoices, and other documentation of expenses and income. This will ensure that all relevant deductions and credits are properly documented.

Keep the tax professional informed of any changes in the investment strategy, such as the acquisition or sale of a property. This will allow the tax professional to adjust the tax strategy as needed.

Review tax returns carefully before filing to ensure that all relevant deductions and credits have been properly documented. This will reduce the risk of errors or omissions on the tax return.

Work with the tax professional to plan ahead for future tax obligations, such as capital gains taxes and depreciation recapture. This will ensure that these obligations are properly accounted for in the investment strategy.

Working with a qualified tax professional is essential for maximizing the profitability of multi-family real estate investments while minimizing tax liability. When selecting a tax professional, consider their experience, qualifications, communication skills, and fees. It is important to establish a productive working relationship and keep accurate records, communicate regularly, review tax returns, and plan ahead for future tax obligations. With the guidance of a qualified tax professional, investors can achieve their financial goals and build a successful multi-family real estate investment portfolio.

CHAPTER TWENTY TWO

Exit Strategies

Investing in multi-family real estate can provide a stable income stream, long-term appreciation potential, and significant financial benefits. However, it is essential to have a solid exit strategy in place to maximize profits and minimize risks. In this chapter, we will discuss the most common exit strategies for multi-family real estate investments, including their benefits and drawbacks, and how to effectively execute them.

Different investors have their own preferences for different strategies. The reasons are as varied as the number of different investors out there and they have their own reasons for their preferences. Whether it is the strategy that is easiest for them, the only strategy that they've ever tried or only one they ever learned. Carefully consider the different strategies and decide on the one that is right for you. Consider your strategy when you are evaluating the property for profitability before you even acquire the property. Remember, just because you think you want one go with one strategy when you acquire your investment property, doesn't mean that is the strategy that you have to use. What might seem like the best strategy at any particular time may not be the best strategy when you are ready to exit your investment. You can change your mind. Choose the exit strategy that works best for you. For me, it is always the one that puts the most money into my pocket.

Developing a Plan for Selling or Refinancing

As an investor in multi-family real estate, the ultimate goal is to maximize returns on your investment. Many investors enter into their multi-family investment with the intention of selling or refinancing. This often involves carefully planning your exit strategy, whether it be selling the property or refinancing it to leverage its equity. Develop a comprehensive plan for selling or refinancing multi-family real estate investments.

Sell the Property

Selling the property is one of the most common exit strategies for multi-family real estate investments. When the property is sold, investors can realize a profit on their investment and use the proceeds to reinvest in other properties or allocate the funds elsewhere. Remember, the buyer of your property is also going to be an investor. If they are informed, they will be evaluating all of the same things you do when you acquired the property. Make sure that your property is an appealing purchase. Unfortunately, too many investors try to boost the income of their property just before they plan to sell it. These same strategies could have been implemented when they owned the property to put more money into their pockets for the duration of their ownership.

To maximize profits when selling the property, investors should consider market conditions, property condition, and timing. Working with a qualified real estate agent who has experience in selling multi-family properties can be invaluable. They can help determine the best time to sell, prepare the property for sale, and ensure that the property is marketed effectively to attract potential buyers.

It is important to note that selling a property can also trigger significant tax consequences, including capital gains taxes. Investors should work with a qualified tax professional to ensure that they are properly accounting for taxes and minimizing tax liability. We'll discuss some strategies for dealing with capital gains in this same chapter.

Refinance the Property

Refinancing the property is another common exit strategy for multi-family real estate investments. By refinancing, investors can take advantage of lower interest rates and free up cash to reinvest in the property or other investments. A common strategy and one that I have often utilized myself is refinancing the equity out of properties, especially ones that have been owned for a while. Equity is not considered profit so you don't pay tax on equity. There are so many different things you can do with this equity that you've now pulled out of your property but that could literally be a whole other book. One of the things I like to use equity that has been cashed out of properties is to invest it into other properties. The interest rate for a refinance is usually a little lower than for a purchase. By paying down the note with a bigger down payment, I am paying less interest on the note. I will have more equity in the property which I can also cash out in a few years to repeat the process and though my ROI might be lower, the actual income from the property will be greater.

Refinancing can also help investors increase cash flow by lowering monthly mortgage payments with lower interest rates.

A refinance can also provide additional capital for property improvements or other investments.

When refinancing, investors should carefully consider the costs associated with refinancing, such as closing costs and fees. It is also important to ensure that the new mortgage terms are favorable and align with the investor's investment goals.

Hold the Property

This strategy is my personal favorite. Remember earlier when I said I prefer the strategy that puts the most money into my pocket? For myself, I'm in this for the long game. My preference is to hold a property for cash flow and appreciation. This is the strategy that has historically put the most money into my pockets. When I evaluate my own multi-family purchases, I do so with this strategy in mind. Holding onto the property and collecting rental income is a long-term exit strategy for multi-family real estate investments. This strategy is ideal for investors who are looking for a stable income stream and long-term appreciation potential.

When holding the property, investors should ensure that the property is properly maintained and managed. This can include regular maintenance and repairs, updating amenities and appliances, and maintaining good tenant relationships.

Holding the property can also provide tax benefits, such as the ability to deduct expenses and depreciation from taxable income. Investors should work with a qualified tax professional to ensure that they are maximizing tax benefits and minimizing tax liability.

1031 Exchange

A lot of investors seem to be fixated on this strategy for whatever reason. Just because you are deferring taxes doesn't mean you are getting the most out of your money. I see a lot of uninformed investors choosing this strategy strictly for the tax benefit and exchanging properties that have decent cash flows for properties that have inferior cash flows.

A 1031 exchange is a tax-deferred exchange that allows investors to sell a property and reinvest the proceeds in another property without paying capital gains taxes. This strategy is ideal for investors who are looking to defer taxes and reinvest in a property that aligns with their investment goals. Though this strategy has the word "exchange" built into the title, it isn't exactly one investor exchanging a property with another investor.

To take advantage of a 1031 exchange, investors must follow strict IRS guidelines and work with a qualified intermediary. The intermediary holds the proceeds from the sale of the property and reinvests them in the replacement property. Investors must also identify the replacement property within 45 days of the sale of the original property and complete the exchange within 180 days.

It is important to carefully consider the replacement property and ensure that it aligns with the investor's investment goals. A 1031 exchange can be a complex process, and investors should work with a qualified tax professional and intermediary to ensure compliance with IRS regulations.

Having an exit strategy in place is essential for maximizing the profitability of multi-family real estate investments. Whether you choose to sell the property, refinance, hold onto it, or pursue a 1031 exchange, it is important to carefully consider the market conditions, property condition, and your investment goals.

Investors should work with a qualified real estate agent, tax professional, and financial advisor to ensure that their exit strategy aligns with their investment goals and maximizes profitability while minimizing tax liability

Investing in multi-family real estate can provide significant financial benefits, but it is essential to have a well-planned exit strategy in place to ensure that you maximize your profits and achieve your investment goals. An exit strategy is a plan that outlines how you will exit the investment, whether it is through selling the property, refinancing it, holding it long-term, or pursuing a 1031 exchange. Though a 1031 Exchange can be a good option in the right situation. Have a talk with your tax professional about reinvestment of capital gains. As a general rule of thumb, reinvesting capital gains within a certain period of time into many other investments is typically a tax deferred occurrence. For example, if you cash out your stocks and the profits from your stocks and invest it into a multi-family property, you don't pay taxes on the capital gains from those stocks. The IRS will wait until you sell your multi-family property investment for a profit and tax that profit. By speaking with your tax professional and the right planning, you can legally offset and minimize your tax burden.

Assessing the Market and Property

Before making any decisions about selling or refinancing your multi-family property, it is crucial to assess the current market conditions and the performance of your investment. Consider the following factors:

Market Analysis

Conduct a thorough analysis of the local real estate market to determine the demand for multi-family properties, rental rates, vacancy rates, and the overall economic outlook. Look for indicators that suggest whether it is a buyer's or seller's market. Analyze recent market trends and forecasts to gauge future potential.

Property Performance

Evaluate the performance of your multi-family property by analyzing its cash flow, occupancy rates, rental income, and expenses. Consider the property's historical performance as well as its potential for future growth. Assess any necessary improvements or upgrades that could enhance its value and appeal to potential buyers or lenders. Also, if you are considering a 1031 Exchange or reinvesting your capital gains from the sale of your property, make sure that the investment you are acquiring will produce more profit that the one your are liquidating.

Capitalization Rate and Comparable Sales

We discussed CAP rate as a tool for determining value. Calculate your property's capitalization rate (cap rate) to determine its value based on its net operating income (NOI). Additionally, research recent comparable sales in the area to gauge the property's market value. This information will help you set an appropriate asking price or assess the property's potential for refinancing.

Define Your Investment Goals

To develop a sound plan for selling or refinancing, you need to clarify your investment goals. Determine what you aim to achieve and the timeframe you have in mind. Are you looking to cash out and realize a profit, or do you intend to reinvest the proceeds into another real estate venture? Clearly define your objectives to guide your decision-making process. Establishing specific goals will help you determine whether selling or refinancing aligns better with your long-term investment strategy.

Consult Professionals

Engaging the expertise of real estate professionals can provide invaluable insights and guidance throughout the selling or refinancing process. Consider consulting the following experts:

Real Estate Agent or Broker

A seasoned real estate agent or broker with experience in multi-family properties can assist you in pricing your property accurately, marketing it effectively, and negotiating with potential buyers. They can also provide market trends and advice based on their knowledge of the local real estate market. A reputable agent can attract qualified buyers or lenders, ensuring a smooth transaction.

Real Estate Attorney

Seek the counsel of a real estate attorney to review contracts, legal documents, and assist with any legal implications associated with the sale or refinance. They can ensure compliance with all applicable laws and regulations. An attorney will safeguard your interests and help navigate any potential legal complexities involved in the process.

Accountant or Financial Advisor

Consult with an accountant or financial advisor to evaluate the tax implications and financial impact of selling or refinancing your investment. They can help you optimize your investment strategy to minimize tax liabilities and maximize returns. Additionally, they can assess the financial viability of refinancing options, comparing them to potential returns from a sale.

Consider Financing Options

When deciding between selling or refinancing, carefully consider the available financing options and their potential benefits or drawbacks. This analysis will help you make an informed decision based on your investment goals and current market conditions. Some financing options to consider include:

Traditional Refinance

Explore the possibility of refinancing your property by securing a new loan with more favorable terms, such as a lower interest rate, longer repayment period, or improved cash flow. This option allows you to retain ownership of the property while accessing its equity. Analyze the potential impact on monthly cash flow and the long-term financial benefits before deciding on this option.

Cash-Out Refinance

If you need capital for other investments or expenses, a cash-out refinance allows you to tap into your property's equity and receive a lump sum payout. However, be mindful of the potential increase in mortgage payments and associated costs. Evaluate the overall financial impact and the viability of reinvesting the funds in a more profitable venture.

Seller Financing

In a buyer's market or if you're having trouble finding qualified buyers, consider offering seller financing as an option. This strategy involves providing a loan to the buyer, allowing them to make payments directly to you instead of securing traditional financing. Evaluate the creditworthiness of potential buyers and assess the risks associated with carrying the financing yourself. Consider seeking legal advice to draft a comprehensive agreement that protects your interests.

Marketing and Preparing the Property for Sale

If you decide to sell your multi-family property, effective marketing and property preparation are vital for attracting potential buyers and maximizing your selling price. Consider the following steps:

Property Enhancement

Assess the property's condition and identify any necessary repairs or upgrades to enhance its appeal. Enhancing curb appeal, refreshing common areas, and improving unit interiors can significantly increase its market value. Determine a budget for renovations and consider the return on investment for each improvement.

Staging

Present the property in its best light by staging it appropriately. Furnish common areas and model units to showcase the lifestyle and potential of the property. Professional staging can help potential buyers envision themselves living in the space and increase their emotional connection to the property.

Professional Photography and Virtual Tours

Hire a professional photographer to capture high-quality images of the property's exterior, interior, and amenities. In today's digital age, virtual tours are increasingly popular. Utilize 3D virtual tours or video walk-throughs to provide potential buyers with an immersive experience of the property, even from a distance.

Marketing Strategy

Develop a comprehensive marketing strategy to reach potential buyers. Leverage both online and offline channels, including listing the property on reputable real estate websites, utilizing social media platforms, and engaging local real estate networks. Consider targeted marketing efforts to attract investors or buyers interested in multi-family properties.

Open Houses and Showings

Schedule open houses and private showings to allow interested parties to visit the property. Ensure the property is well-maintained and presentable during these events. Respond promptly to inquiries and provide comprehensive information to potential buyers.

Developing a plan for selling or refinancing your multi-family real estate investment requires a thorough assessment of the market, property performance, and your investment goals. Consulting professionals, considering financing options, and implementing effective marketing strategies are key components of a successful exit strategy. By carefully analyzing the available options and developing a comprehensive plan, you can maximize the returns on your multi-family real estate investment while aligning with your long-term investment objectives.

Identifying Market Conditions That May Affect the Sale of an Investment Multi-Family Property

When considering the sale of an investment multi-family property, it is essential to thoroughly understand the market conditions that may impact the selling process. The real estate market is dynamic and subject to various factors that can influence property values, buyer demand, and overall market activity. In this chapter, we will explore in-depth the key market conditions to consider when assessing the potential sale of a multi-family property.

Economic Factors

Economic conditions play a crucial role in the real estate market. Analyzing these factors will help you understand the overall health of the economy and its impact on the sale of your investment property. Consider the following:

Employment and Job Growth

The strength of the local job market and employment opportunities can significantly influence the demand for rental properties. Areas with robust job growth and low unemployment rates tend to attract more renters, increasing the market demand for multi-family properties. Conversely, areas with high unemployment rates or job losses may experience reduced demand.

GDP and Economic Growth

The overall economic growth of a region, as measured by the Gross Domestic Product (GDP), can impact property values and investor sentiment. Strong economic growth often translates into increased demand for real estate investments, including multi-family properties. Economic downturns, on the other hand, may lead to decreased demand and lower property values.

Interest Rates and Financing Availability

Fluctuations in interest rates can affect the affordability of mortgages and influence buyer demand. Lower interest rates generally stimulate real estate activity, making it more attractive for buyers to invest in properties. Additionally, the availability of financing options can impact the number of potential buyers in the market. Tighter lending standards or limited access to credit can reduce buyer demand.

Supply and Demand Dynamics

Understanding the supply and demand dynamics in the multi-family property market is crucial for gauging the market conditions that may affect the sale of your investment property.

Inventory Levels

Assess the current supply of multi-family properties in your area. A high inventory level can indicate increased competition, potentially leading to a longer time on the market and potentially lower selling prices. Conversely, low inventory levels may create a seller's market, with higher demand and the potential for quicker sales and favorable prices.

Rental Market Trends

Analyze rental market trends, such as vacancy rates, rental rates, and tenant demand. Strong rental demand and low vacancy rates generally indicate a healthy market, increasing the likelihood of attracting potential investors or buyers for your multi-family property. On the other hand, high vacancy rates or declining rental rates may indicate a less favorable market for sellers.

Development Activity

Monitor the level of new construction and development activity in the multi-family sector. Increased development may lead to a higher supply of available units, potentially impacting market rents and the overall demand for existing properties. An oversupply of multi-family units can affect the competitiveness of your property in the market.

Demographic Factors

Demographic factors can provide insights into the target market for multi-family properties and their preferences. Analyze the following demographics to assess the potential demand for your investment property:

Population Growth

Evaluate the population growth rate in your area. Regions experiencing population growth may have increased demand for housing, including rental properties. Growing populations, particularly in urban areas, often lead to a higher demand for multi-family properties.

Household Formation

Changes in household formation patterns, such as an increase in single-person households or multi-generational households, can influence the demand for multi-family properties. Understanding the evolving demographics can help position your property to cater to specific target markets. For example, properties with flexible layouts or amenities suitable for families or young professionals may attract a larger pool of potential buyers.

Lifestyle Preferences

Consider the preferences and lifestyle choices of the target demographic. Factors such as proximity to amenities, public transportation, schools, and employment centers can significantly impact the marketability of your multi-family property. Urban areas with convenient access to transportation and amenities often attract younger professionals and families seeking a convenient lifestyle.

Local Market Trends and Competition

Stay informed about local market trends and the competitive landscape. Research comparable sales, rental rates, and market conditions specific to your neighborhood or sub-market. Understanding the strengths and weaknesses of competing properties can help you position your investment property effectively and set a competitive asking price.

Comparable Sales

Research recent sales of similar multi-family properties in your area to determine the market value. Analyze the sale prices, time on the market, and any unique features that contributed to their success. This information will help you price your property competitively.

Rental Market Analysis

Study rental rates and vacancy rates for similar multi-family properties in the area. Evaluate the demand for various unit sizes and amenities to determine the rental income potential and market attractiveness of your property.

Market Trends

Stay updated on local market trends, such as shifts in demand, new developments, or changes in zoning regulations that may impact the multi-family property market. Understanding these trends will help you adapt your selling strategy and effectively position your property.

Identifying market conditions that may affect the sale of an investment multi-family property requires a comprehensive analysis of economic factors, supply and demand dynamics, demographic trends, and local market trends. By thoroughly evaluating these factors, you can gain valuable insights into potential buyer demand, pricing strategy, and marketing approach. A comprehensive understanding of market conditions allows you to make informed decisions, optimize your property's value, and maximize returns on your investment.

CHAPTER TWENTY THREE

Investing in Emerging Markets

As the real estate market becomes increasingly competitive, many investors are exploring opportunities in emerging markets for multi-family properties. Emerging markets offer the potential for high returns, favorable economic conditions, and untapped growth opportunities. However, investing in these markets requires careful analysis, due diligence, and a thorough understanding of the unique challenges and dynamics at play. This chapter provides an extensive and detailed exploration of investing in emerging markets for multi-family properties, equipping you with the knowledge and strategies to navigate these markets successfully.

Understanding Emerging Markets

Before diving into the specifics of investing in emerging markets for multi-family properties, it's important to understand what defines an emerging market. Emerging markets are economies that exhibit rapid economic growth, transitioning from a developing to a developed state. These markets typically have favorable demographics, expanding middle-class populations, improving infrastructure, and increasing urbanization.

Investing in emerging markets requires thorough market research and analysis to identify the most promising opportunities.

Economic and Political Stability

Assess the economic and political stability of the emerging market. Look for countries with sound governance, favorable investment policies, and stable economic indicators.

Demographics and Urbanization

Analyze the demographics of the market, including population growth, urbanization rates, and the size of the middle class. A growing population and increasing urbanization indicate a higher demand for multi-family properties.

Supply and Demand Dynamics

Evaluate the supply and demand dynamics of the multi-family property market in the emerging market. Look for indicators such as low vacancy rates, rising rental rates, and a limited supply of quality properties.

Infrastructure Development

Consider the level of infrastructure development in the market, including transportation, utilities, and amenities. Developing infrastructure supports the growth potential of multi-family properties.

Economic Indicators

Study economic indicators such as GDP growth, inflation rates, interest rates, and employment levels. Positive economic indicators indicate a favorable investment climate.

Legal and Regulatory Environment

Understand the legal and regulatory environment in the emerging market. Familiarize yourself with property ownership laws, taxation policies, and any restrictions or regulations on foreign investors.

Risk Assessment and Mitigation

Investing in emerging markets carries inherent risks. It's crucial to assess and mitigate these risks to protect your investment. Consider the following risk factors:

Currency and Exchange Rate Risk

Fluctuations in currency exchange rates can impact the value of your investment. Implement strategies such as hedging or diversifying your currency exposure to mitigate this risk.

Political and Regulatory Risk

Political instability or changes in regulations can adversely affect your investment. Stay informed about the political climate and maintain a contingency plan to navigate any potential challenges.

Market Liquidity

Emerging markets may have less liquidity compared to more established markets. Understand the implications of limited liquidity and have strategies in place to manage potential challenges in buying or selling properties.

Local Market Knowledge

Lack of local market knowledge can pose risks. Partner with local professionals who have expertise in the market to gain insights, navigate local regulations, and identify investment opportunities.

Due Diligence

Conduct thorough due diligence on properties, sellers, and local partners. Verify property ownership, assess property condition, and scrutinize financials to ensure the viability and profitability of your investment.

Building Local Relationships

Establishing strong relationships with local stakeholders is vital in emerging markets. These relationships can provide valuable market insights, access to off-market deals, and a network of reliable partners. Attend local real estate events, engage with industry professionals, and cultivate relationships with local property managers, brokers, and legal advisors.

Risk Diversification

Diversify your investment portfolio to mitigate risks associated with investing in emerging markets. Consider investing in multiple properties across different emerging markets or diversifying across asset classes to balance your risk exposure.

Exit Strategies

Develop clear exit strategies for your investments in emerging markets. Consider options such as selling properties to local investors, partnering with local developers, or leveraging the property's cash flow to fund further investments.

Investing in emerging markets for multi-family properties offers exciting opportunities for growth and high returns. However, it requires careful research, analysis, risk assessment, and relationship-building. By understanding the dynamics of emerging markets, conducting thorough due diligence, mitigating risks, and establishing strong local relationships, you can capitalize on the potential of these markets and achieve long-term success in your multi-family property investments. Remember to continuously monitor market conditions, adapt your strategies, and stay informed to navigate the unique challenges and opportunities presented by emerging markets.

CHAPTER TWENTY FOUR

Investing in Sustainable and Green

In an era marked by pressing environmental challenges, sustainable and green living has emerged as a paramount concern for individuals, businesses, and communities worldwide. Real estate investors, recognizing the importance of incorporating environmentally-friendly practices into their portfolios, are increasingly turning their attention to investing in sustainable and green multi-family properties. This article delves into the advantages of investing in these properties, highlighting the financial benefits and responsible decision-making that underpin such investments.

Positive Environmental Impact

Investing in sustainable and green multi-family properties or updating older multi-family properties with sustainable and green options offers significant opportunities to potentially cut costs while making a tangible difference in reducing carbon emissions and promoting environmental sustainability. These properties integrate energy-efficient technologies and sustainable practices that significantly reduce their carbon footprint. For instance, implementing solar panels, LED lighting, energy-efficient appliances, and smart home automation systems minimizes energy consumption and reliance on fossil fuels. Additionally, sustainable property management practices such as rainwater harvesting, greywater recycling, and green landscaping contribute to the preservation of natural resources. By prioritizing these initiatives, investors actively contribute to a healthier and more sustainable future for both residents and the planet.

Lower Operational Costs

One of the most compelling advantages of investing in sustainable multi-family properties is the potential for reduced operational and maintenance costs. Energy-efficient technologies and sustainable practices lead to lower utility expenses, resulting in increased cash flow and higher profitability. By integrating renewable energy sources such as solar panels, geothermal heating and cooling systems, and energy-efficient insulation, property owners can generate their own electricity and reduce dependence on conventional energy sources. Subsequently, this reduces energy bills, increasing the property's profitability. Similarly, water-saving fixtures, low-flush toilets and drought-resistant landscaping reduce water consumption, lowering water bills. These cost-saving measures not only benefit the property's bottom line but also make it more attractive to potential tenants.

Rising Demand for Sustainable Housing

As sustainability awareness grows, there is an increasing demand for sustainable housing options. Millennial's and Gen Z, in particular, actively seek eco-friendly living spaces that align with their values. Investing in multi-family properties that prioritize sustainability and green features positions investors at the forefront of this growing market. By meeting the demand for environmentally-conscious housing, property owners can attract high-quality tenants who are willing to pay a premium for sustainable features. This leads to lower vacancy rates, increased rental income, and greater overall property value. As sustainability becomes an essential criteria for housing choices, investing in sustainable multi-family properties provides a competitive advantage in the rental market.

Government Incentives and Regulations

Governments at various levels are actively promoting sustainable initiatives and offering incentives for property owners who adopt green practices. These incentives can take the form of tax credits, grants, or subsidies for implementing energy-efficient systems or sustainable construction methods. By investing in sustainable multi-family properties, investors can tap into these financial incentives, further enhancing the profitability of their investments. Additionally, several jurisdictions are implementing stricter regulations regarding energy efficiency and environmental standards for buildings. By proactively investing in sustainable properties, investors position themselves ahead of these regulations, reducing the risk of costly retrofits in the future and ensuring compliance with evolving sustainability standards.

Enhanced Property Value and Long-Term Returns

Sustainable and green multi-family properties tend to have higher property values due to their lower operational costs, reduced environmental impact, and increasing demand. Investors can expect higher resale values, especially as sustainability becomes a standard requirement in the real estate market. The marketability and desirability of these properties are likely to increase over time. Furthermore, sustainability initiatives often lead to long-term cost savings, which translate into higher returns on investment. By considering the total cost of ownership, including operational expenses and potential increases in utility costs, investors can make informed decisions that maximize their returns over time.

Identifying Opportunities for Sustainable Multi-Family Investing

Investing in sustainable and green multi-family properties is not only an ethically responsible choice but also a lucrative investment strategy. By focusing on reducing environmental impact, lowering operational costs, meeting rising demand, and capitalizing on government incentives, investors can enjoy long-term financial rewards while contributing to a sustainable future. As the world continues to prioritize environmental stewardship, sustainable properties are likely to become even more attractive to investors and tenants alike. By investing in sustainable multi-family properties, investors can secure both financial returns and contribute to a sustainable future for generations to come.

Investing in sustainable multi-family properties presents a unique opportunity to combine financial success with environmental responsibility. However, identifying the right opportunities in this niche market requires a comprehensive understanding of the key factors that contribute to sustainable and profitable investments. Consider the essential considerations and strategies for identifying opportunities for sustainable multi-family investing in greater detail.

Evaluate Existing Properties for Sustainability Improvements

An effective approach to sustainable multi-family investing is evaluating existing properties that have the potential for sustainability improvements. Look for properties that may require energy-efficient upgrades, such as outdated HVAC systems, inefficient insulation, or outdated appliances. These properties present an opportunity for value-add investing, where you can enhance sustainability and increase property value simultaneously.

Consider conducting energy audits and sustainability assessments to identify areas for improvement. Evaluate the potential for implementing renewable energy sources, such as solar panels or geothermal systems, and assess the property's suitability for water-saving fixtures and landscaping. Additionally, consider the feasibility and cost-effectiveness of installing energy-efficient lighting and appliances. These upgrades can lead to reduced operating costs, increased tenant satisfaction, and improved property value.

Explore New Construction and Development Projects

Another avenue for sustainable multi-family investing is through new construction and development projects. Identify regions with a growing demand for rental housing and a strong emphasis on sustainable living. Collaborate with architects and contractors who specialize in sustainable design and construction to develop energy-efficient and environmentally-friendly properties.

Consider incorporating sustainable features such as green roofs, rainwater harvesting systems, energy-efficient building materials, and smart home automation. Additionally, research sustainable building certifications, such as LEED (Leadership in Energy and Environmental Design) or ENERGY STAR, as they can enhance the marketability and value of your development.

Build Partnerships and Networks

Building strong partnerships and networks can greatly facilitate the identification of opportunities for sustainable multi-family investing. Connect with professionals in the real estate industry who specialize in sustainability, such as green architects, property managers, and contractors. Collaborate with sustainability-focused organizations and attend industry conferences and events to stay informed about emerging trends and opportunities.

Additionally, consider partnering with financial institutions that offer green financing options. These institutions may provide favorable loan terms and incentives for sustainable projects, reducing your financing costs and increasing the feasibility of your investments.

Engage with the Community and Align with Stakeholders

Engaging with the local community and aligning with stakeholders is essential when investing in sustainable multi-family properties. Understand the needs and preferences of potential tenants in the area. Conduct surveys or engage in community discussions to gain insights into their sustainability priorities and incorporate them into your investment strategy.

Additionally, build relationships with local government agencies, environmental organizations, and community groups. Collaborate with them to ensure your investment aligns with local sustainability.

Identifying opportunities for sustainable multi-family investing requires a comprehensive approach that encompasses market research, property evaluation, new construction, partnerships, and community engagement. By thoroughly assessing the market, evaluating existing properties, considering new construction projects, and building strong networks, investors can uncover opportunities that offer both financial returns and environmental impact. By aligning financial goals with sustainability, investors contribute to a greener future while generating profitable returns from their investments.

Evaluating the benefits and risks of sustainable investing

Evaluating the benefits and risks of sustainable investing is crucial for investors who are interested in aligning their financial goals with environmental, social, and governance (ESG) considerations. Sustainable investing, also known as socially responsible investing (SRI), seeks to generate positive financial returns while promoting sustainable practices, addressing societal challenges, and mitigating environmental risks. In order to make informed investment decisions, it is important to assess the potential benefits and risks associated with this approach.

Benefits of Sustainable Investing

Sustainable investing offers the opportunity to contribute to positive social and environmental change. By investing in companies that prioritize sustainable factors, investors can support businesses that align with their values and promote sustainability goals.

Sustainable investing encourages companies to adopt responsible business practices, which can help mitigate various risks. Companies that prioritize sustainability are often at the forefront of innovation. Sustainable investing can provide access to companies involved in developing cutting-edge technologies, such as renewable energy, clean technology, and resource efficiency, which may offer long-term growth opportunities.

Risks of Sustainable Investing

Sustainable investing strategies can result in varied investment performance. Some studies indicate that certain sustainable investment approaches may under-perform compared to traditional investment strategies, especially in the short term. It is important for investors to conduct thorough research and consider their investment horizon when evaluating potential risks.

Green-washing refers to the misleading or exaggerated claims made by companies regarding their sustainability practices. Some companies may overstate their sustainability efforts to attract socially conscious investors, while their actual practices may not align with their claims.

The regulatory and policy landscape surrounding sustainable

investing is evolving. Changes in regulations, shifts in government priorities, or a lack of consistent standards could impact the performance and viability of sustainable investments. Investors should stay informed about relevant regulations and policy developments to mitigate potential risks.

Evaluating the benefits and risks of sustainable investing is essential for investors aiming to incorporate sustainability factors into their investment decisions. While sustainable investing offers the potential for positive impact, long-term performance, risk mitigation, and access to innovative opportunities, it is important to consider potential performance variations, limitations, and regulatory uncertainties.

CHAPTER TWENTY FIVE

Investing in Affordable Housing

The availability of affordable housing is a critical issue worldwide, affecting individuals, families, and communities. In this chapter we'll explore the importance of investing in affordable housing, the challenges associated with it, and the potential benefits for us as investors and society as a whole.

Public Housing

Public housing is the oldest and, until recently, largest housing subsidy program in the United States. Today's 1.1 million plus units of public housing, operated by over 3,000 local public housing agencies, serve 2.2 million residents. Not to be confused with other housing subsidy programs, public housing is housing stock that is owned by HUD and administered by local PHAs. The federal public housing program started as part of the Housing Act of 1937, passed during the New Deal. First intended to be a jobs program and slums-clearing effort, public housing was the result of powerful grassroots organizing. Social justice advocates like Catherine Bauer of the Regional Planning Association of America mobilized massive public support for the movement for government-sponsored housing. The passing of the Housing Act of 1949, significantly increased the number of public housing agencies (PHAs) and led to more widespread construction of the public housing stock we see today.

Fair Housing Act passed in 1968 and just six years later the federal government started a steady withdrawal of support for public housing beginning with President Nixon's moratorium on housing spending in 1974. There has been no significant expansion of public housing since then, as federal housing subsidies shifted to housing vouchers.

Government Subsidized Housing

Subsidized housing is government sponsored economic assistance aimed towards minimizing housing costs and expenses for impoverished people with low to moderate incomes. In the United States, subsidized housing is often called "affordable housing". Forms of subsidies include direct housing subsidies, non-profit housing, public housing, rent supplements/vouchers, and some forms of co-operative and private sector housing.

This investment strategy can be an internal struggle for many investors and initially I had my own struggles with it myself. I grew up believing that anyone can pull themselves up by their own bootstraps and I had been able to do that for myself and I knew of others who had as well. I personally felt that subsidizing housing, income, anything, removes a persons motivation and enables them to continue in poverty. There are even a number of studies that support this. The thought of being part of this was a bit of a personal struggle. In the end, I realized that regardless of whether I condoned these programs or not, these programs are a reality and I am being forced by the Federal Government to fund these programs with my tax dollars. The wise business decision for me was to recoup my tax investment and profit from it. After all, this was money that was being taken from me to support these programs that I didn't agree with. The least I could do was to try and get my money back along with a profit.

In the more than three decades that I have been investing in Section 8 properties, I've come to some epiphanies. Many of my original opinions of the program were correct. There are many people in the Section 8 program that are scammers and liars. They drive expensive cars, wear expensive clothes, even have expensive furniture and electronics in their government subsidized unit. There are however people who do need the assistance and I am glad I was able to be a part of that process. I have had amazing Section 8 tenants who were physically and mentally disabled, who were veterans and single parents struggling to provide for their children. My way of thinking about government subsidies came around to a degree. I still believe that anyone can pull themselves up with their own bootstraps but I realize that sometimes, people just need a hand and sometimes, lending a hand allows someone to move themselves forward.

I've now been investing in government subsidized, low-income housing for decades and it has been very profitable for me. These types of properties currently make up the majority of my portfolio.

Housing subsidies are government funded financial assistance programs designed to mitigate the costs of housing for low-income tenants. Subsidies can be provided in the form of housing vouchers given to tenants. This is typically done through Housing Choice vouchers or via direct deposits to landlords with government contracts to provide affordable housing. There are various types of government subsidized housing, Section 8 Housing Choice Vouchers, Low-Income Housing Tax Credits (LIHTC), and other rental assistance programs. Each program operates differently, but their common goal is to ensure that low-income households have access to safe, decent, and affordable housing.

Some additional housing subsidies are provided to low income tenants for rental housing. These include shelter allowances, housing supplements, and shelter supplements from regional and local governments designed to help low-income households that spend a large proportion of their income on rent. One such program is New York City's Family Eviction Prevention Supplement program. The subsidies are often defined by whether the subsidy is given to the landlord and then criteria are set for the tenants they can lease to or whether the subsidy is given to the tenant, typically as a voucher, and they are allowed to find suitable private housing. The subsidy amount is typically based on the tenant's income, usually the difference between the rent and 30% of the tenant's gross income, but other formulas have been and are still used and they vary from area to area.

As investors, we can profit from these government subsidized programs if we understand them and put ourselves into the right position to do so.

Section 8 Housing Choice

Federal Housing Programs started in the Great Depression. Section 8 of the Housing Act of 1937 (42 U.S.C. § 1437f), often called Section 8, as repeatedly amended, authorizes the payment of rental housing assistance to private landlords on behalf of low-income households in the United States.

In the 1960s and 1970s, the federal government created subsidy programs to increase the production of low-income housing and to help families pay their rent. In 1965, the Section 236 Leased Housing Program amended the U.S. Housing Act. This subsidy program, the predecessor to the modern Section 8 Housing Choice program, was not a pure housing allowance program. Housing authorities selected eligible families from their waiting list, placed them in housing from a master list of available units, and determined the rent that tenants would have to pay. The housing authority would then sign a lease with the private landlord and pay the difference between the tenant's rent and the rate for the same size unit in that market. In the agreement with the private landlord, housing authorities agreed to perform regular building maintenance and leasing functions for Section 236 tenants, and annually reviewed the tenant's income for program eligibility and rent calculations.

Fort Lauderdale, Florida Housing Authority Director William H. Lindsey, upon the advice of Housing Authority attorney J. Richard Smith, initially developed 11(b) financing in the early 1970s to accommodate a local savings and loan interested in assisting with urban renewal projects. Lindsey eventually brought this program to fruition. This was the initial impetus for the subsequent development of the now well known Section 8 Program. 68% of total rental assistance in the United States goes to seniors, children, and those with disabilities. The U.S. Department of Housing and Urban Development (HUD) manages Section 8 programs and they are administered at the local level.

The Housing Choice Voucher Program provides "tenant-based" rental assistance, so a tenant can move from one unit of at least minimum housing quality to another. Of the 5.2 million American households that received rental assistance in 2018, approximately 2.2 million of those households received a Section 8 Housing Choice voucher. Landlords are not required to participate in the voucher program. Some states such as California have laws that prevent landlords from discriminating based on source of income as long as the income meets the minimum requirements to lease the premises. These laws are not applicable in all areas, and the program remains voluntary in most places. The program also allows individuals to apply their monthly voucher towards the purchase of a home, with over $17 billion going towards such purchases each year. Voucher amounts vary depending on city or county, size of unit, and other factors. Once individuals receive a voucher they have a limited amount of time, usually 2 to 4 months, to find a unit with a willing landlord that meets HUD housing standards. If they don't find housing, they lose their voucher and must apply again.

One of the reasons this strategy works so well for investors is the demand. As of 2020, the average wait lists for Section 8 vouchers are very long. The national average is 2 and a half years and in some states can be up to 10 to 20 years. Many city or county programs are permanently closed to new applicants because there isn't enough housing. As of 2022, the national average is a 64% deficit in available housing for Section 8 with the cities of New York, Los Angeles and Miami ranking in the top three.

Voucher amounts are based on Fair Market Rents (FMRs) calculated in the local market by the Department of Housing and Urban Development (HUD). Recently, a Small Area Fair Market Rents (SAFMRs) program was established to reduce the area that rents are based on to the area of zip codes in major metropolitan areas.

Section 8 also authorizes a variety of "project-based" rental assistance programs, under which the owner reserves some or all of the units in a building for low-income tenants in return for a federal government guarantee to make up the difference between the tenant's contribution and the rent amount in the owner's contract with the government. A tenant who leaves a subsidized project will lose access to the project-based subsidy.

The United States Department of Housing and Urban Development (HUD) and the United States Department of Veterans Affairs (VA) have created a program called Veterans Affairs Supportive Housing (VASH), or HUD-VASH, which distributes roughly 10,000 vouchers per year at a cost of roughly $75 million per year to eligible homeless and otherwise vulnerable U.S. armed forces veterans. This program was created in 2008 to pair HUD-funded vouchers with VA-funded services such as health care, counseling, and case management.

In the 1970s, when studies showed that the worst housing problem afflicting low-income people was no longer substandard housing, but the high percentage of income spent on housing, Congress passed the , further amending the U.S. Housing Act of 1937 to create the Section 8 Program. In the Housing and Community Development Act of 1974Section 8 Program, tenants pay about 30 percent of their income for rent, while the rest of the rent is paid with federal money.

The Section 8 program initially had three subprograms—New Construction, Substantial Rehabilitation, and Existing Housing Certificate programs. The Moderate Rehabilitation Program was added in 1978, the Voucher Program in 1983, and the Project-based Certificate program in 1991. The number of units a local housing authority can subsidize under its Section 8 programs is determined by Congressional funding. Since its inception, some Section 8 programs have been phased out and new ones created, although Congress has always renewed existing subsidies.

The Housing and Urban Development Act of 1970 introduced the federal Experimental Housing Allowance Program (EHAP) and the Community Development Corporation and authorized larger outlays for housing subsidy programs and rent supplements for moderate-income households.

The 2008 Consolidated Appropriations Act (Public Law 110-161) enacted December 26, 2007, allocated $75 million in funding for the HUD-Veterans Affairs Supportive Housing (HUD-VASH) voucher program, authorized under section 8(o)(19) of the United States Housing Act of 1937. This new program combines HUD Housing Choice Voucher rental assistance for homeless veterans with case management and clinical service support which is provided by the

Veterans Affairs administration at its own medical centers and also in the community.

Investing in Government Subsidized Housing

Investing in government-subsidized housing provides an opportunity for real estate investors to generate stable returns while fulfilling a social purpose. There are clearly a number of different ways that an investor could benefit from acquiring properties with the intention of making them available for government subsidized housing. I'm going to cover the strategies that are most common.

Government-subsidized housing are residential properties that receive financial assistance from government programs to make housing affordable for low-income individuals and families.

One of the greatest benefits of investing in government subsidized housing is the steady cash flow that it provides. Government subsidies ensure consistent rental income, as a portion of the rent is paid directly by the government or through housing vouchers. Government-subsidized housing typically comes with long term contracts, ensuring stable occupancy and income streams for the investor. The government subsidized portion of your rent is paid directly to you or your property manager (your choice) on or before the first of each month by the Federal Government.

Since the demand for affordable housing often exceeds supply, this results in lower vacancy rates and a reduced risk of prolonged periods without tenants.

Investing in government-subsidized housing allows investors to contribute to the community by providing safe and affordable housing options to low-income individuals and families.

Consider utilizing low-income housing tax credits (LIHTCs) available through the LIHTC program, which can attract investors and provide additional financing for affordable housing projects. Low-Income Housing Tax Credits (LIHTCs) are a federal tax incentive program designed to encourage the development and preservation of affordable rental housing for low-income individuals and families. LIHTCs provide dollar-for-dollar reductions in federal income tax liability for investors in affordable housing. These tax credits can be used directly by the investor or sold to generate capital. Specifics for this program vary by area and the government agency administering the program. Typically, by making a certain portion of units if not all available for low income or housing voucher tenants, the owner of the property qualifies for low income housing tax credits. This can often be done while still making a profit on rents.

Collaborate with experienced property management companies and consultants with expertise in government-subsidized housing programs in your market to navigate the complexities and maximize returns.

Develop positive relationships with local community organizations, government entities, and social service providers to foster support and create a sense of community within the subsidized housing property.

Investing in government-subsidized housing requires adherence to specific regulations and program guidelines set by the governing agency. Familiarize yourself with these regulations to ensure compliance. The agency inspects your property prior to approving it for their program and the will regularly inspect the property to make sure that it is in compliance with their requirements. The agency will accept the property unless it has passed their inspection and during their regular inspection, if they find an issue, it must be quickly remedied.
Government-subsidized housing programs may require periodic renewals or approvals. Stay updated on program changes and maintain a proactive approach to secure continued participation and funding.

Effective property management is crucial for maintaining the quality of subsidized housing units and complying with program standards. Budget for ongoing maintenance and ensure effective tenant communication and support.

Conduct thorough research and due diligence on the specific government-subsidized housing program, property location, tenant demographics, and financial projections.

Section 8 Housing Choice Voucher

Investing in properties for Section 8 tenants offers an opportunity to generate steady, consistent rental income as the government directly pays a portion of the rent on behalf of the tenant. This means a considerably lower risk of tenant default: With the government's involvement, the risk of tenant non-payment is reduced, providing more stability and predictability for landlords.

Rents for Section 8 properties are determined by the local Pic Housing Authority (PHA) based on fair market rents and the tenant's income. Understanding the rent determination process will help ensure that the property's rental income is in line with program guidelines. Understand the calculation of rental income for Section 8 properties based on program guidelines, tenant contributions, and subsidy payments. Accurate income calculations are essential for financial planning and rent collection.

You can research the different types and amounts for housing vouchers in any particular market in the websites of the PHA for that market. One of the first steps an investor interested in this strategy should take it to contact the PHA and have a conversation with them. These conversations are often very informative. PHA employees can let you know the demand for Section 8 Housing in their market, requirements and how to get the process started to become a Section 8 landlord. Another great move is to contact a local property management company that specializes in managing Section 8 properties in that market. By having the right information, you are able to fine tune your investing strategy. For example, in some markets, a three bedroom unit is valued considerably higher than a two bedroom unit. In this situation, it makes more financial sense to try and acquire properties with 3 bedroom units. In other markets, a two bedroom unit and a three bedroom unit are valued nearly the same. In this case, it makes more sense to acquire properties with two bedroom units as they are probably more affordable that properties with three bedroom units and you are also likely saving on factors such as maintenance, insurance and property tax. Know your market.

Develop a comprehensive budget that considers expenses such as property maintenance, repairs, property management fees, insurance, and property taxes. Proper budgeting ensures the property remains financially sustainable.

Properties participating in the Section 8 program must meet specific housing quality standards and pass inspections conducted by the local Public Housing Authority (PHA). Familiarize yourself with these standards and ensure compliance to maintain eligibility for the program. Maintaining the property in good condition is crucial to comply with program requirements and retain Section 8 tenants. Promptly address maintenance issues and make necessary repairs to provide safe and habitable housing.

By understanding the Section 8 program, property eligibility requirements, tenant screening processes, financial considerations, and implementing effective property management strategies, investors can navigate this specialized market and achieve successful and sustainable investments. With careful planning, diligent property management, and compliance with program guidelines, investing in Section 8 properties can yield consistent rental income and contribute to meeting the affordable housing needs of low-income individuals and families.

Investing in LIHTC Properties

Low-Income Housing Tax Credits are federal tax incentives provided to developers and investors who finance the construction or rehabilitation of affordable rental housing projects. LIHTCs are allocated by state agencies and allow investors to claim tax credits over a period of years.

There are primarily two different LIHTC programs. The 9% LIHTC program provides a 9% tax credit, resulting in more significant equity financing for the development of affordable housing projects. The 4% LIHTC program offers a 4% tax credit, typically used in conjunction with tax-exempt bond financing to support the development or preservation of affordable housing.

Investing in LIHTC properties allows developers to attract equity investors who are seeking tax benefits and are interested in supporting affordable housing initiatives. This equity financing can help reduce the reliance on debt and improve the financial viability of the project.

LIHTC properties typically provide stable rental income due to long-term affordability restrictions and strong demand for affordable housing. This stability reduces the risk of tenant turnover and vacancy, ensuring consistent cash flow for investors.

Investing in LIHTC properties requires compliance with specific program guidelines, including rent restrictions, tenant income eligibility, and ongoing monitoring and reporting. Familiarize yourself with these requirements to ensure ongoing compliance.

If you are just starting out with this strategy, partner with experienced developers and property management companies with a track record of successfully developing and managing LIHTC properties. Their expertise can help navigate the complexities of the program and ensure compliance.

Understand that LIHTC properties are subject to rent restrictions to ensure affordability for low-income tenants. Understanding these restrictions and accurately calculating rental income is essential for financial planning and compliance.

Develop a comprehensive financial plan that considers construction or rehabilitation costs, debt financing, equity investment, and the value of the tax credits. Proper financial planning ensures the project's viability and long-term sustainability. Account for ongoing operating expenses, such as property maintenance, management fees, insurance, utilities, and reserves for unexpected expenses. Proper budgeting is essential to maintain the property's financial health.

Consider partnering with tax credit syndicators who specialize in assembling investors and managing the LIHTC process. Syndicators can provide expertise in structuring the investment and managing compliance requirements.

Thoroughly research the LIHTC property, including the development team's track record, the location's demand for affordable housing, market conditions, and potential risks. Conducting proper due diligence minimizes potential pitfalls and enhances the chances of success.

Develop a comprehensive asset management plan to ensure ongoing compliance with LIHTC regulations, oversee property operations, and monitor financial performance. Regular reviews and reporting help identify and address any compliance or operational issues.

By understanding LIHTCs, considering the benefits, compliance requirements, and implementing effective financial and asset management strategies, investors can navigate the complexities of LIHTC investments and make a positive social impact. Successful investment in LIHTC properties requires careful planning, collaboration with experienced developers, ongoing compliance monitoring, and a commitment to providing safe and affordable housing for low-income individuals and families.

Investing in government-subsidized housing offers both financial and social benefits. Understanding the various government programs, conducting thorough due diligence, complying with regulations, and implementing effective property management strategies are key to successful investment in this sector. By considering the benefits, challenges, and specific risk factors associated with government-subsidized housing, investors can make informed decisions and profit while providing safe, affordable housing options for those in need.

CHAPTER TWENTY SIX

Investing in Distressed Properties

Getting a property that is turn key and ready to go is great but for me, I find it very satisfying to rehab a property and put my fingerprints all over it. Investing in distressed multi-family properties can be an excellent opportunity for real estate investors looking to capitalize on undervalued assets. In this chapter we'll cover the advantages, challenges, due diligence, and potential exit strategies for distressed multi-family properties.

Distressed properties refer to real estate assets that are in financial or physical distress. In the context of multi-family properties, this can include buildings facing foreclosure, high vacancy rates, significant maintenance or management issues, or other financial difficulties. These properties often offer attractive investment opportunities due to their lower market value and the potential for value appreciation.

Advantages of Investing in Distressed Multi-Family Properties

Distressed properties are typically sold below their market value, providing investors with an opportunity to acquire assets at a discounted price. This lower purchase price can increase the potential for higher returns on investment.

Distressed multi-family properties often require renovations, improvements, or repositioning to maximize their value. Investors can implement value-added strategies such as improving property management, upgrading units, enhancing amenities, or addressing deferred maintenance. These enhancements can increase rental income and property value.

Multi-family properties, even distressed ones, tend to benefit from consistent rental demand. People will always need affordable housing, and investing in distressed multi-family properties in areas with robust rental markets can provide a stable income stream.

Perform a thorough financial analysis of the distressed multi-family property before making an investment. Evaluate the property's income and expense statements, rent rolls, vacancy rates, and operating costs. Assess the property's potential income after implementing value-add strategies to determine its profitability.

Conduct a detailed physical inspection of the property to assess its condition and identify any necessary repairs or renovations. Pay close attention to the structural integrity, mechanical systems, roofing, plumbing, and electrical systems. Engage professionals such as contractors, inspectors, and engineers to ensure a comprehensive evaluation.

Review the property's legal and title documents to identify any potential issues or encumbrances. This includes examining liens, outstanding debts, zoning restrictions, and compliance with local regulations. Engage a real estate attorney to guide you through the due diligence process.

Analyze the local market dynamics, including supply and demand for multi-family properties, rental rates, occupancy rates, and neighborhood trends. Consider factors such as proximity to amenities, transportation, schools, and employment centers. A thorough market analysis will help determine the property's potential for rental income growth and appreciation.

Financing and Acquisition Strategies

Explore financing options for acquiring distressed multi-family properties, such as traditional bank loans, private lenders, hard money loans, or partnerships with other investors. Consider the property's condition, your financial capacity, and the projected return on investment when selecting the most suitable financing option.

Negotiate with the property owner or the lender holding the distressed property to secure favorable terms. Be prepared to present your offer based on the property's current condition, potential value-add opportunities, and market comparables. Engage a real estate agent or broker experienced in distressed property transactions to assist with negotiations.

Develop a strategic exit plan before acquiring a distressed multi-family property. Potential exit strategies may include selling the property after implementing value-add strategies, refinancing to extract equity, or holding the property for long-term rental income. Evaluate market conditions and investor goals to determine the most suitable exit strategy.

Managing and Rehabilitating Distressed Properties

Rehabilitating distressed multi-family properties can be a lucrative investment strategy that involves renovating and improving the condition of under performing or dilapidated properties.

Rehabilitating distressed multi-family properties allows investors to create value by improving the property's physical condition, amenities, appearance and overall appeal. This value creation can result in increased rental income, higher property values, and potential appreciation.

By renovating and upgrading units and common areas, investors can attract higher-quality tenants and command higher rental rates. Rehabilitated properties often offer improved living spaces and amenities, which can justify higher rents in the market.

Rehabilitating distressed multi-family properties helps position them competitively within the local market. Upgraded properties with modern features and amenities have a greater chance of attracting tenants and maintaining high occupancy rates.

Rehabilitation efforts can address deferred maintenance, structural issues, and other property-related challenges. By preserving and enhancing the property's condition, investors can ensure its long-term stability, reduce ongoing maintenance costs, and protect the asset's value.

Thoroughly assess the property's current condition, identifying areas that require repair, renovation, or improvement. Engage professionals such as contractors, architects, and engineers to evaluate the property and develop a detailed scope of work. The scope of work should outline specific tasks, materials, timelines, and budget estimates.

Develop a comprehensive budget that considers all the necessary repairs, renovations, and improvements. Include costs for materials, labor, permits, professional services, and contingencies. Ensure that the budget is realistic and aligns with the expected return on investment.

Determine the permits and approvals required for the rehabilitation project. Consult with local building departments, zoning authorities, and other relevant agencies to ensure compliance with regulations and obtain the necessary permits before commencing any work.

Create a detailed timeline that outlines the sequence of work and sets realistic deadlines for each phase of the rehabilitation project. Properly managing the timeline ensures efficient execution and minimizes delays, ultimately reducing carrying costs and maximizing returns.

Select experienced and reputable contractors, subcontractors, and vendors to carry out the rehabilitation work. Seek recommendations, review portfolios, and obtain multiple quotes to ensure quality workmanship, cost-effectiveness, and adherence to timelines.

Focus on completing essential repairs and upgrades that address safety concerns, building code violations, and structural integrity first. This may include fixing plumbing and electrical issues, repairing roofs, replacing windows, and ensuring compliance with accessibility regulations.

Renovate individual units by updating kitchens, bathrooms, flooring, and fixtures. Consider incorporating modern design elements and energy-efficient features to attract tenants. Enhance common areas, such as lobbies, hallways, laundry facilities, and recreational spaces, to provide a more appealing and functional living environment.

Identify value-added opportunities that can further enhance the property's appeal and profitability. This may include adding amenities like fitness centers, communal outdoor spaces, or co-working areas. Consider leveraging technology by installing smart home features or offering high-speed internet connectivity.

Implement effective property management practices to address any existing operational challenges and improve tenant satisfaction. This may involve enhancing tenant screening procedures, implementing efficient maintenance systems, and establishing clear communication channels with residents.

Develop a targeted marketing strategy to attract tenants to the rehabilitated property. Utilize online platforms, social media, local advertising, and partnerships with real estate agents to promote the property's improved features, amenities, and value proposition.

Focus on building positive tenant relationships to promote tenant satisfaction and retention. Provide excellent customer service, address tenant concerns promptly, and regularly maintain and upgrade the property to ensure tenant comfort and satisfaction.

Rehabilitating distressed multi-family properties can be a rewarding investment strategy that creates value, increases rental income, and positions the property competitively in the market. Proper planning, thorough assessment, realistic budgeting, efficient execution, and successful property management are key to a successful rehabilitation project. By revitalizing distressed properties, investors can unlock the potential for long-term stability, profitability, and asset appreciation..

Investing in distressed multi-family properties requires careful evaluation, due diligence, and strategic planning. By understanding the advantages, conducting thorough due diligence, implementing value-added strategies, and managing the property rehabilitation effectively, investors can capitalize on the opportunities presented by distressed assets. With proper research and execution, investing in distressed multi-family properties can yield attractive returns and contribute to a well-diversified real estate investment portfolio.

Future Outlook

As real estate investors, we also need to be able to predict the future. Fortunately, we have a number of tools that help us with this and based upon definitive historical trends and what we can observe for ourselves currently, we can usually make pretty reasonable predictions. The multi-family real estate sector is experiencing a transformative period, shaped by various factors such as technological advancements, changing tenant preferences, demographic shifts, and sustainability considerations. This chapter delves into the trends and developments that I believe are set to define the future of multi-family real estate in greater detail.

Technology without a doubt is a part of our every day life and is becoming more an more integrated into every aspect of our lives and that includes real estate and real estate investing. Finding and using these technologies as tools to benefit our investing efforts is going to be essential in order for us as investors to be competitive and profitable. Integrating technologies into our investment properties is also going to be key in keeping our properties in competitive demand and positioning our properties for future technological enhancements.

The integration of IoT devices is revolutionizing multi-family properties. Smart home technology, including smart thermostats, lighting systems, security features, and appliances, offers convenience, energy efficiency, and enhanced security for tenants. Property owners are increasingly adopting these technologies to attract tech-savvy residents and optimize property management operations.

AI and machine learning are playing a significant role in multi-family real estate. Property management software powered by AI algorithms can automate routine tasks such as rent collection, maintenance scheduling, and tenant screening. These technologies also facilitate predictive analytics, helping property owners and managers make data-driven decisions on rental rates, lease renewals, and tenant retention strategies.

VR and AR technologies are transforming the way multi-family properties are marketed and showcased to potential tenants. Virtual tours and immersive experiences allow prospects to explore units and communal spaces remotely, improving the efficiency of the leasing process and attracting a wider audience.

Modern tenants are seeking more than just a place to live—they desire a community and lifestyle. Properties that offer appealing amenities such as state of the art fitness centers, co-working spaces, rooftop gardens, pet-friendly facilities, and communal lounges foster a sense of community and enhance the tenant experience.

The demand for flexible lease terms and customizable living spaces is growing. Short-term leases, furnished units, and co-living arrangements cater to a mobile and diverse tenant base in many markets. Property owners who can adapt to these evolving preferences will have a competitive edge in attracting and retaining tenants.

The COVID-19 pandemic has heightened awareness of health and well-being considerations. Tenants are increasingly seeking properties with features that prioritize cleanliness, indoor air quality, and wellness amenities. This includes touchless technology, air filtration systems and activities that don't require tenants to leave home such as fitness centers, yoga studios, and outdoor recreational areas.

Urbanization continues to drive demand for multi-family properties, particularly in vibrant urban centers with job opportunities and amenities. Millennials, the largest renter demographic, are drawn to the convenience, affordability, and social aspects of multi-family living. Properties located in desirable locations and designed to cater to their preferences will experience sustained demand.

The aging population presents opportunities for multi-family properties tailored to the needs of seniors. Active adult communities with age-friendly amenities, healthcare services, and social activities are in high demand. Accessibility features, health-focused designs, and convenient access to medical facilities can cater to the unique requirements of seniors.

The drive towards sustainability and energy efficiency will continue to shape the future of multi-family real estate. Building codes and regulations are likely to become more stringent, incentivizing property owners to invest in energy-efficient systems, renewable energy sources, green building certifications, and sustainable materials.

The future of multi-family real estate is being shaped by technological advancements, evolving tenant preferences, demographic shifts, and sustainability considerations. Embracing IoT, AI, VR, and AR technologies will optimize property management and enhance tenant experiences. Offering desirable amenities, flexibility, and health-conscious features will attract and retain tenants. Understanding the needs of urban dwellers, Millennials, and the aging population will guide location and design decisions.

www.ingramcontent.com/pod-product-compliance
Lightning Source LLC
Chambersburg PA
CBHW070619220526
45466CB00001B/62